WITHDRAWN
No longer the property of the
Boston Public Library.
Sale of this material benefits the Library.

SHIPS

Crossing the World's Oceans

These and other books are included in the Encyclopedia of Discovery and Invention series:

Airplanes

Anesthetics

Animation

Atoms

Clocks

Computers

Genetics

Germs

Gravity

Human Origins

Lasers

Microscopes

Movies

Phonograph

Photography

Plate Tectonics

Printing Press

Radar

Railroads

Ships

Telephones

Telescopes

Television

Vaccines

SHIPS
Crossing the World's Oceans

by SEAN M. GRADY

The ENCYCLOPEDIA of
D·I·S·C·O·V·E·R·Y
and **INVENTION**

P.O. Box 289011 San Diego, CA 92198-9011

Copyright 1992 by Lucent Books Inc., P.O. Box 289011,
San Diego, California, 92198-9011

No part of this book may be reproduced or used in any other
form or by any other means, electrical, mechanical, or otherwise,
including but not limited to photocopy, recording, or any
information storage and retrieval system, without prior written
permission from the publisher.

Library of Congress Cataloging-in-Publication Data

Grady, Sean M., 1965-
  Ships: crossing the world's oceans / Sean M. Grady.

    p. cm.—(The Encyclopedia of discovery and invention)
  Includes bibliographical references and index.
  Summary: Discusses the history and development of the
ship, its influence on trade, types of ships, and the future of
the ship.
  ISBN 1-56006-220-7
  1. Ships—History—Juvenile literature.   2. Navigation—
History—Juvenile literature. [1. Ships—History.]   I. Title.
II. Series.
VM150.G68 1992
387.2—dc20
                                                           92-9162

Contents

■■

Foreword

The belief in progress has been one of the dominant forces in Western Civilization from the Scientific Revolution of the seventeenth century to the present. Embodied in the idea of progress is the conviction that each generation will be better off than the one that preceded it. Eventually, all peoples will benefit from and share in this better world. R.R. Palmer, in his *History of the Modern World*, calls this belief in progress "a kind of nonreligious faith that the conditions of human life" will continually improve as time goes on.

For over a thousand years prior to the seventeenth century, science had progressed little. Inquiry was largely discouraged, and experimentation, almost nonexistent. As a result, science became regressive and discovery was ignored. Benjamin Farrington, a historian of science, characterized it this way: "Science had failed to become a real force in the life of society. Instead there had arisen a conception of science as a cycle of liberal studies for a privileged minority. Science ceased to be a means of transforming the conditions of life." In short, had this intellectual climate continued, humanity's future would have been little more than a clone of its past.

Fortunately, these circumstances were not destined to last. By the seventeenth and eighteenth centuries, Western society was undergoing radical and favorable changes. And the changes that occurred gave rise to the notion that progress was a real force urging civilization forward. Surpluses of consumer goods were replacing substandard living conditions in most of Western Europe. Rigid class systems were giving way to social mobility. In nations like France and the United States, the lofty principles of democracy and popular sovereignty were being painted in broad, gilded strokes over the fading canvasses of monarchy and despotism.

But more significant than these social, economic, and political changes, the new age witnessed a rebirth of science. Centuries of scientific stagnation began crumbling before a spirit of scientific inquiry that spawned undreamed of technological advances. And it was the discoveries and inventions of scores of men and women that fueled these new technologies, dramatically increasing the ability of humankind to control nature—and, many believed, eventually to guide it.

It is a truism of science and technology that the results derived from observation and experimentation are not finalities. They are part of a process. Each discovery is but one piece in a continuum bridging past and present and heralding an extraordinary future. The heroic age of the Scientific Revolution was simply a start. It laid a foundation upon which succeeding generations of imaginative thinkers could build. It kindled the belief that progress is possible as long as there were gifted men and women who would respond to society's needs. When Antonie van Leeuwenhoek observed *Animalcules* (little animals) through his high-powered microscope in 1683, the discovery did not end there. Others followed who would call these "little animals" bacteria and, in time, recognize their role in the process of health and disease. Robert Koch, a German bacteriologist and winner of the Nobel Prize in Physiology and Medicine, was one of these men. Koch firmly established that bacteria are responsible for causing infectious diseases. He identified, among others, the causative organisms of anthrax and tuberculosis. Alexander Fleming, another Nobel Laureate, progressed still further in the quest to understand and control bacteria. In 1928, Fleming discovered penicillin, the antibiotic wonder drug. Penicillin, and the generations of antibiotics that succeeded it, have done more to prevent premature death than any other discovery in the history of humankind. And as civilization hastens toward the twenty-first century, most agree that the conquest of van Leeuwenhoek's "little animals" will continue.

The *Encyclopedia of Discovery and Invention* examines those discoveries and inventions that have had a sweeping impact on life and thought in the modern world. Each book explores the ideas that led to the invention or discovery, and, more importantly, how the world changed and continues to change because of it. The series also highlights the people behind the achievements—the unique men and women whose singular genius and rich imagination have altered the lives of everyone. Enhanced by photographs and clearly explained technical drawings, these books are comprehensive examinations of the building blocks of human progress.

SHIPS
Crossing the World's Oceans

SHIPS

Introduction

Although the first boats were built around 8000 B.C., it was not until much later that explorers ventured beyond the coastline out into the open sea. Without reliable ships, these early people believed the ocean and the world were vast and unknown and full of danger, strange creatures, and mystery. Without a way to cross the oceans, people were bound by land travel and short-distance exploration by water.

But the possibility of commerce with other nations, coupled with the desire for exotic riches, led people to build bigger and bigger boats. These boats gradually developed into the ships of the ancient Egyptians, Phoenicians, and other societies. However, these ships almost never ventured out over the deep ocean.

Finally, in the fifteenth century, shipbuilders living near the Mediterranean built what many historians consider the

... TIMELINE: SHIPS

1 > 2 > 3 > 4 > 5 > 6 > 7 > 8 > 9 > 10 > 11 > 12 > 13 > 14

1 ■ Before 3500 B.C.
Human beings learn how to travel on water in boats.

2 ■ 3500 B.C.
Egyptian boatmen on the Nile River invent the square sail. About the same time, sailors in Indonesia invent the triangular sail.

3 ■ 1200 to 333 B.C.
Phoenician merchant ships control most of the trade in the Mediterranean Sea.

4 ■ 600 B.C.
A Phoenician ship makes the world's first voyage around Africa.

5 ■ 300 B.C. to A.D. 475
Rise, dominance, and fall of the Roman Empire.

6 ■ 793 to 1000
Period of Viking raids and voyages of exploration.

7 ■ 986
Viking captain Bjarni Herjulfsson becomes the first European to see North America.

8 ■ 1407
Chinese admiral Cheng Ho leads a fleet of ships on the first of seven voyages around the Indian Ocean.

9 ■ 1420
Portugal's Prince Henry the Navigator begins the search for a trade route to India; development of the caravel.

10 ■ 1450
Development of the carrack.

11 ■ 1492
Christopher Columbus comes across the Americas while looking for a western sea route to China.

12 ■ 1498
Portugese explorer Vasco da Gama reaches India by sailing around Africa.

13 ■ 1500 to 1600
Dominance of world sea trade by Spain and Portugal. Development of the galleon.

14 ■ 1595
Development of the Dutch trading ship, the *fluyt*.

first sailing ships that were capable of long voyages out of sight of land. These ships, and those that were developed after them, allowed people to explore and map every part of the world. At the same time, ships gave people the means to invade other nations and exploit them for gold, silver, and slaves.

Ships continue to be an important part of commerce, travel, and war. Most of the world's trade is carried out using cargo ships. Warships can both strike at an enemy during war and patrol the world's shipping lanes during peacetime. And some ships have been built as seagoing vacation super resorts.

Ships chronicles the story of the men and women who gazed to the far horizon, dreaming of crossing to unknown lands. And it shows how individual ingenuity, determination, and bravery made the invention and the use of these tools of human progress possible.

16 17 18 19 20 21 22 23 24 25 26

15 ■ 1684
Emperor K'ang-hsi opens Chinese ports to foreigners after more than two hundred years of Chinese isolation. Beginning of British tea trade.

16 ■ 1768
Captain James Cook sails on his first exploration of the Pacific Ocean.

17 ■ 1807
Robert Fulton's *Clermont* becomes the world's first successful commercial steamship.

18 ■ 1838
Great Western, a British passenger ship, becomes the second steamship to cross the Atlantic Ocean. It arrives in New York Harbor a few hours after a steam-powered Irish coastal steamer, the *Sirius*.

19 ■ 1843
Beginning of the golden age of the clipper ship. *Great Britain* becomes the first oceangoing steamship with an iron hull and screw propellers.

20 ■ 1884
Charles Parsons invents the steam turbine engine.

21 ■ 1897
Rudolf Diesel invents the diesel engine.

22 ■ 1907
Cunard liner *Mauretania* captures the record for the fastest sailing time across the Atlantic.

23 ■ 1935
Maiden voyage of the superliner *Normandie*. In 1942, the ship burns and capsizes while being converted into a troop carrier.

24 ■ 1960
Development of the container ship.

25 ■ 1980s
The Japanese coastal tanker *Shin Aitoku Maru* proves that sail-assisted ships can be run economically.

26 ■ 1985
Maiden Voyage of Jacques-Yves Cousteau's turbosail ship *Alcyone*.

To Cross the Water

Anthropologists and archaeologists—scientists who study the development of human cultures—cannot say when the first journey off a lakeshore or riverbank might have taken place. They can only say that people have been traveling on the water since before 8000 B.C. The first artifacts of early boat-building societies—remains of fishing villages, tools made of rocks found only on certain islands, and primitive boats themselves—date from after that time. From these artifacts, scientists can tell that people had been experimenting with water travel before 8000 B.C.

Rafts and Canoes

Archaeologists think people began making vessels to travel on the water at least ten thousand years ago. The earliest watercraft were rafts and dugout canoes. Rafts were usually made from logs that were lashed together, but other materials were used if logs were in short supply. Along Egypt's Nile River and in South America, reeds were tied into log-shaped bundles. These bundles were used by themselves or were tied together for added stability and cargo space. In China, bamboo stalks were used to make rafts that curved up at the front, or bow, and the back, or stern.

People living in what is today northern Iraq and eastern Turkey developed a particularly successful river raft that was made of inflated animal skins tied to an open framework of logs or smaller poles. River traders floated their goods downstream on these rafts. When they reached their destination, the traders took the raft apart. They sold the poles and lashings along with their trade goods. They then deflated the skin floats and carried them upstream on donkeys. When the traders had a new load of goods to sell, they built a new raft and sailed downstream. Both Herodotus, a Greek historian who lived

Herodotus, a historian who lived in Greece during the fifth century B.C., once traveled on a raft made from inflated animal skins.

in the fifth century B.C., and Sir Austen Layard, a nineteenth-century British archaeologist, used this type of raft on their travels.

Often, people who used rafts also used canoes or canoelike boats. Dugout canoes, which were made by hollowing out a tree trunk, have been found throughout the world. Archaeologists found one such canoe in the Netherlands that dated back to 6500 B.C. Ancient stone tools that have been found suggest that large dugouts were used in northern Europe and areas near the Mediterranean Sea before this time.

Other societies built canoes out of different materials. North American Indians made canoes out of tree bark sewn into a boat shape around a wooden frame. The Eskimo developed canoes made of skins also sewn to a wooden framework. These canoes developed into the single-person kayak and a large fishing boat known as the umiak. Skin-and-framework boats were also used by people in the British Isles and in the Middle East.

Rafts changed only slightly over the

Early Indians often made canoes using tree bark or skins sewn to a wooden frame.

next few thousand years. Some of the most advanced rafts were developed in Egypt. There, as many as five reed bundles were sewn together to make a curved, boat-shaped platform. For extra strength, the rear end of the raft was often bent forward to tighten the structure.

Canoes, on the other hand, evolved into more complex forms. Dugout builders found ways of making their craft larger. They discovered they could widen the body of the dugout by heat-

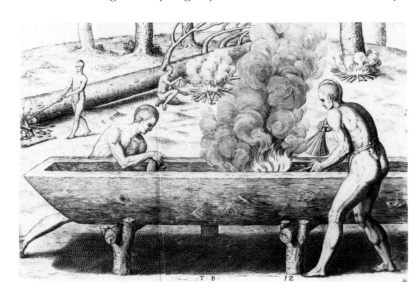

Many types of early boats were made from hollowed-out tree trunks.

ing it over a low fire. The heat made the sides of the boat soft enough to flatten out. They also found that forcing one or two planks of wood across the inside of the boat made the craft stronger and better able to retain its shape.

Wooden planks were also added to the sides of the boat to keep out water and to create more space for cargo. The planks were either sewed or nailed into the side of the boat. Eventually, boat builders decided not to hollow out the bottom log of the boat. They simply nailed the side planks, called strakes, onto the log to make the boat's body. This bottom support log became the main support of all boats and ships and is called the keel.

Experiments in Egypt

From 4000 to 3000 B.C., only two factors were keeping boats from becoming ships—size and power. Of these two factors, the biggest problem was power. At first, the only available power source was human labor. Boats could only go as far as their rowers were strong enough to take them. Then, sailors be-

gan experimenting with ways to capture and tame the wind.

By examining paintings on the walls of ancient Egyptian tombs, archaeologists believe the first sail was developed by the Egyptians around 3500 B.C. The sail was a large, rectangular sheet of cloth that powered small reed-bundle boats upstream along the Nile River. Egyptian sailors attached the top edge of this cloth to a long pole. The lower corners were tied with rope to the rear of the boat. To hold up the cloth, the top pole was hung from a vertical support, called a mast, at the front of the boat. The Egyptian mast was made of two poles joined at the top, with a supporting crossbar halfway down. This A shape allowed the mast to straddle the rounded bundles of reeds that made the boat.

These first sails were mounted well in front of a boat's midsection and were set up with the sail hanging straight across the width of the ship. Unfortunately, the boat's sail was useful only when the wind blew from the rear. In nautical terms, this meant the boat could only sail "before the wind."

Even with this drawback, sails still

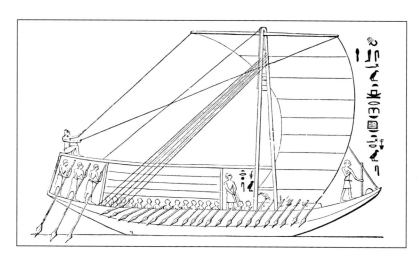

This Egyptian boat has the characteristic rectangular sail, held up with a vertical support called a mast.

As travel by boat became more common, Egypt extended its power and influence to other countries. This Phoenician boat, with its large square sail, was most likely modeled after the Egyptian design.

made a major impact on trade and politics in the eastern Mediterranean. By 3200 B.C., Egypt had large, wooden, sail-equipped boats sailing north from the mouth of the Nile. These early sea voyages were raiding expeditions, ordered by the pharaohs to demonstrate Egypt's might. The raiders brought back food, jewels, and other goods as well as slaves and political prisoners who could be held for ransom.

As time went on, the Egyptians began building larger boats with wood imported from the upper Nile and the eastern Mediterranean. These vessels carried a large square sail on a single-pole mast. The sail itself was rigged so that it could be turned to catch wind blowing from the side of the craft.

By 2500 B.C., these boats were big enough to be considered small ships, although they still were not true ocean-going ships. They rarely lost sight of a coastline. And a boat's crew usually had to ground the vessel each night in order

to cook dinner and to sleep. Still, these ships allowed Egypt to attain both economic and military power. As Egypt extended its power, knowledge of the sail was transferred to other cultures. The kingdom on the island of Crete; Phoenicia, the kingdom based in modern Lebanon; Syria; and Israel; and the empires of Greece and Rome all used ships similar to the ones the Egyptians invented.

Sails in the Pacific

There is some disagreement over whether the Egyptians were the first to invent the sail. Some scholars believe that people living in the Indonesian islands developed their own sail around the same time the Egyptians invented theirs. Archaeological excavations throughout the South Pacific and legends of Pacific Island societies seem to support this theory. The Indonesian sail was slightly different from the Egyptian version. Instead of a square shape, the Indonesians used a triangular sail. The point of the triangle rested at the bottom of a mast that was a single vertical pole. Because the inverted-triangle design could capture a wider range of wind, it allowed the Indonesians to travel to Asia and other islands in the Pacific Ocean.

As the Indonesians traveled, other cultures were exposed to the idea of sail travel. One group, the Polynesians, created unusual-looking vessels that some argue were the first true oceangoing ships. These craft, called *tainui*, looked like modern catamarans. Two dugout canoes, each seventy feet long, were joined by a large wooden deck. This deck usually had a large cabin for supplies or the ship's crew. The most impressive thing about the tainui, though,

Some argue that the Polynesian tainui *was the first true ocean-going ship. It had two claw-shaped sails to catch the wind.*

was its two sails. They had the inverted-triangle shape of the Indonesian sail, but they looked like giant crab claws, with their pincers pointing to the open sky.

China, however, became a major Asian shipping power because of a ship called the junk. The junks were powered by a lugsail. This sail was shaped like a trapezoid, a triangle with its top point chopped off. The sheet of the sail was strengthened by a series of bamboo battens, strips of wood sewn into the sail. The battens kept the sail stiff when it was raised. This stiffness allowed the sail to make use of very light gusts of wind.

The lugsail was so efficient at using small breezes that Chinese sailors compared it to a human ear that kept listening for the wind. Each junk had three or more lugsails in line with the keel. These sails captured more wind than other sails and could therefore push heavier loads over the seas. The junks could be built to carry more cargo than the ships of the Mediterranean.

Chinese traders gradually took control of the seas east of India around 1000 B.C. By the tenth century A.D., "Chinese ships were probably the biggest and most reliable in the world," according to naval historian J. H. Parry in his book *Romance of the Sea*. In the early fifteenth century, the first of seven fleets of junks sailed all around the Indian Ocean. Yet the skilled Chinese mariners did not become the great explorers of the world. That honor went to the sailors from Portugal, Spain, England, and other western European nations. What held the Chinese back?

For one, Chinese society was organized so that a person's birth and occupation determined his or her status. In

The junk could take advantage of small gusts of wind and was able to carry heavy cargo loads. These advantages helped China become a major Asian shipping power.

this system, intellectuals and bureaucrats were ranked at the top. Merchants, on the other hand, were ranked near the bottom. Decrees from the Chinese emperors kept merchant families from gaining great wealth and high status. As a result, the merchants had no reason to develop their trade routes beyond a certain point.

But the major reason for the lack of Chinese exploration came in 1433. In that year, the ruling Ming emperor declared that contact with foreigners was forbidden. Because the emperor believed that foreign ideas might corrupt the Chinese people, he forbade voyages of trade and exploration. This decree effectively isolated China from the rest of the world. Aside from a small amount of trade in the East Indies, China was a forbidden land to outsiders for more than two hundred years.

East Meets West

Though China did not keep its seagoing fleets after the fifteenth century, it did influence the development of other ships that would circle the globe. As the junks sailed west, they inspired people living in India and Arabia to develop their own sailing ships and boats. Because the junks had roughly triangular-shaped sails, the sails of the Indians and Arabs were generally triangular in shape. There were also practical reasons for using triangular sails. The sail proved very useful in capturing winds that blew over the side of the ship. Most of the winds in the western Indian Ocean blow from the northeast and the southwest. The triangular sails allowed Arabian and Indian ships to sail both east and west.

Some of the ships that sailed west reached the shores of Egypt and the Sinai Peninsula. Merchants and other travelers carried the idea of the triangular sail overland from these ports to the Nile River and the Mediterranean Sea. The sailors of the Mediterranean found that their square sails did not work as well as the new imports from the Far East. Since the triangular sails held the wind more easily than the square sails did, maneuvering was easier. And because the new sails caught winds blowing over the side of a ship as well as from the rear, sailors could travel in more directions than before.

The Vikings

In northern Europe, meanwhile, sailors were still using the square sail. The people responsible for keeping the square sail alive were the Vikings. The Vikings were warrior-seamen who raided the coasts of Europe and Britain in the early Middle Ages. They came from the Scandinavian countries of Norway, Sweden, and Denmark. From roughly the year 793 to 1000, they plundered cities and villages using swift, sail-and-oar-powered vessels called longboats. Their raids carried them as far away as Pisa, Italy, and upstream along rivers like the Thames in England and the Seine in France. They also explored the northern Atlantic Ocean and journeyed to Iceland, Greenland, and even the coast of North America.

The Vikings ceased their raids soon after the tenth century. By that time, Viking rulers dominated the northern

The Vikings used ships to raid and dominate northern European countries.

European countries they had raided. Instead of seeking new lands, the rulers went to war with each other over the lands they had conquered. During the lulls in fighting, however, these nations developed trade routes with each other.

The trade ship these countries used

Viking ships called longboats relied on people to operate the oars and wind to operate the sails.

By adding fighting platforms above the main deck, the cog *could be used as a trading vessel and a warship.*

was a variation of a Viking craft called the *knarr*. The knarr looked like a large, wide longboat without oars. Its freeboard—the distance between a ship's waterline and the top of its hull—was higher than that of the longboats, which meant it could carry more goods. Compared to the sleek, wave-cutting shape of the longboat, the knarr looked tubby. This round shape became more pronounced as the northern Europeans built bigger trade ships.

Within a few hundred years, these ships looked like sail-powered wooden washtubs. The best-known example of these ships was the *cog*, which was used both as a trading vessel and, with a few modifications, as a warship. The modifications involved adding fighting platforms, or castles, to the ship above the main deck. Usually, three castles were used: two large castles in the bow and stern and a smaller one on the mast above the sail. These castles eventually became permanent features: the fore-

castle (pronounced fōk-səl); the stern castle; and the top castle, or "fighting top."

The cog represented the height of shipbuilding in northern Europe. Even so, it was not a deep-ocean craft. Its single sail was good enough for European trade routes, but it only worked well when running before the wind. Cogs generally sailed close to the coastline of the British Isles and mainland Europe. No European sailor even considered an extended voyage unless there was a series of ports within a few days' sailing of each other.

What the sailors of both northern Europe and the Mediterranean Sea needed were ships that could make long voyages using any available wind. They needed a craft that combined the power of the square sail with the versatility of the triangular sail. In short, they needed to merge the cogs of northern Europe with the sailing ships of the Mediterranean.

Sailing the High Seas

There is almost no record of what happened when northern European and Mediterranean shipbuilding came together. But historians know that in the early 1400s, people began building a type of ship that combined features of both. Its hull was deep and U-shaped like the cog's, with a stern-hung rudder, a flat piece of wood that serves as a steering device. But this boat was longer than the typical cog. Large castles stuck out over the bow and stern. This new ship, called a caravel, also used a version of the triangular sail. Northern European sailors associated this type of sail with the Latin-speaking Mediterranean countries. They called it the lateen sail.

Around 1450, shipbuilders began putting large square sails on two masts, one in the middle of the ship and one near the bow. Sometimes, they would put a smaller square sail, called a topsail, above the larger sails. Then, shipbuilders hung a third mast near the stern with a lateen sail. The third mast was called the mizzenmast. Historians think the word *mizzen* came from the Arabic word *mizen*, meaning "balance." Finally, a mast was hung at an angle pointing ahead of the ship's bow. This mast, called a bowsprit, carried a small square or rectangular sail that helped hold the ship in the wind.

This kind of ship was called a carrack. It was the first ship in history capable of making long voyages without in-

The caravel combined some features of northern European and Mediterranean ships. Its square and triangular lateen sails allowed it to sail uninterrupted over long distances, opening the world to Western exploration.

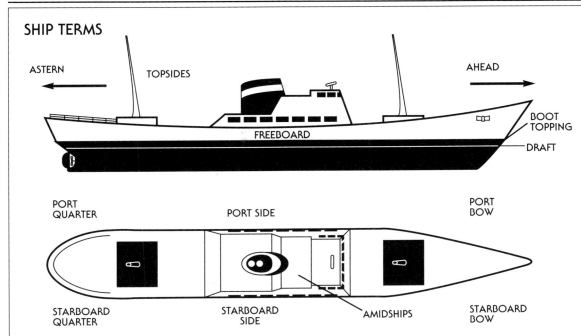

SHIP TERMS

ASTERN

TOPSIDES

AHEAD

BOOT
TOPPING

FREEBOARD

DRAFT

PORT
QUARTER

PORT SIDE

PORT
BOW

STARBOARD
QUARTER

STARBOARD
SIDE

AMIDSHIPS

STARBOARD
BOW

The front of a ship is known as the bow. The rear is the stern. The area halfway between the bow and stern is amidships. The direction toward the bow is forward; the direction toward the stern is aft. Anything in front of the bow is ahead. Anything behind the stern is astern.

The right side of the ship, when facing forward, is the starboard side. The left side, when facing forward, is the port side. The distance from one side of the ship to the other is athwartships. The widest part of the ship is the beam. The direction between the beam and the stern is the quarter.

The way a ship sits in the water is known as the trim. The distance from main deck to the waterline is known as freeboard. The outer surface of the ship above the waterline is called topsides. The paint on the hull of the ship between the load line and the waterline when the boat is empty is the boot-topping. The depth to which the ship sinks in the water is the draft. The slope of the masts or funnel is the rake.

The side of the ship nearest the direction of the wind is the windward side. The side of the ship away from the wind is the leeward side.

terruption. Its square sails could take advantage of virtually any wind. When the wind shifted, its lateen sail kept the ship going while the main sails were readjusted. With its stern-hung rudder and combination of sails, it was the most maneuverable ship in the sea. Although it was a small ship—no more than eighty feet long, as a rule—its

deep hull let it carry more cargo than most other ships of the time.

The carrack soon replaced the cog as the main trading vessel in northern Europe. The caravel, on the other hand, dominated Mediterranean trade. With the use of these two ships, nations finally could travel beyond the range of established port cities. In the fifty years between 1450 and 1500, one nation—Portugal—would use both types of ships to open the world to Western exploration.

Prince Henry and the Age of Discovery

In the 1400s, the Italian port cities of Venice and Genoa dominated Mediterranean sea trade. Venetian and Genoese merchant ships carried most of the food, cloth, and other merchandise sold between the Strait of Gibraltar and the eastern Mediterranean coast. These ships carried spices from the Arab nations of Egypt and Lebanon.

Cloves, cinnamon, ginger, and other spices were more valuable than gold to medieval Europe. Spices masked the flavor of spoiled meat and perked up the taste of other foods. There was no way to preserve meat aside from salting or smoking it, and even then, it usually spoiled. This problem was not too severe during spring and summer, when fresh meat was available. In winter, however, fresh meat was scarce. Farmers killed much of their herd in the fall so they would not have to feed all the animals through the winter.

The spices that made meat and other foods edible were found only in India and the lands of the Far East. Arab merchant ships controlled the spice trade routes across the Indian Ocean. Once the spices reached the ocean's western shore, caravans hauled them to Egypt and Lebanon. Venetian and Genoese merchants then bought the spices and shipped them back to Italy and to other European countries.

Other European nations resented the Italian-Arabian monopoly of the spice trade. They especially resented having to pay the high prices the Italian merchants charged for the spices. Until the 1400s, however, the other nations did not have the knowledge or the ships to find their own trade routes to India and the spice lands.

Prince Henry the Navigator

In 1420, a Portuguese prince named Henry was finally able to challenge the Italian monopoly. Prince Henry, known as the Navigator, was given permission by his father, King John I, to send ships in search of a southern route to the spice lands. Henry knew that merchants from Morocco routinely sent trading caravans east to Egypt. Since land travel across Africa was possible, Henry thought there might be a way across Africa by ship.

Henry thought that a series of rivers

In the fifteenth century Prince Henry sent ships from Portugal to find a trade route to India.

might lead from west to east across Africa. Ships from Portugal could sail along these rivers until they reached the Indian Ocean. If such a route existed, Portugal could begin its own trading monopoly and take power away from the Italian cities.

To seek this trade route, Henry hired the best captains in Portugal and sent them sailing south. The captains had two royal orders to obey. The first order was to find a way from the Atlantic to the Indian Ocean. The second was to find a source of gold the Portuguese could use to buy spices. Although Portugal was a trading nation, it had little gold to spend on spices. And it could not trade European goods for spices, because Asian goods were far superior. Henry told his captains to find either deposits of gold that Portugal could mine or people with gold who were willing to trade it away.

The voyages Henry sponsored did not pay off until after his death in 1460. Though it was a magnificent effort, Portuguese exploration of Africa was slow. The captains had orders to explore every river they found for a possible passage through Africa. The prince had demanded detailed reports and maps of the voyages as well.

After Henry's death, his brother King John II continued to support the search and, between 1460 and 1480, the effort began to pay off. Portuguese explorers found people with grain, ivory, and gold to trade for European goods. These people lived along an area where Africa's west coast curves toward the east. Because of the wealth they found, the Portuguese captains named these areas the Grain Coast, the Ivory Coast, and the Gold Coast.

With the gold supply assured, all

An illustration depicts Portuguese captain Bartholomeu Dias's voyage to the Cape of Good Hope.

that was needed was to find the passage to the Indian Ocean. This feat took an additional seventeen years. In 1488, a Portuguese captain named Bartholomeu Dias sailed a carrack around the stormy Cape of Good Hope at the tip of Africa. The other captains realized they, too, would have to sail around the entire African continent. Dias and his crew set foot on the southeastern coast of Africa to set up a stone cross marking his voyage. He probably knew he had discovered the trade route Prince Henry had sought. His crew, however, balked at the idea of sailing any farther. It was up to another captain to complete the trip into the Indian Ocean.

Portugal's Route to Wealth

In 1497, Vasco da Gama set sail with a fleet of four carracks to attempt the first Portuguese voyage to India. The ships carried goods and gifts that da Gama expected to trade for spices and gold.

Portuguese navigator Vasco da Gama's carrack braved strong winds and dead calms to find a trade route to India.

Only three of the ships were supposed to complete the entire trip. The fourth was a lightly manned supply ship that would be abandoned halfway. Da Gama's voyage marked the first time carracks were used for deep-ocean sailing.

Da Gama knew the trip would be long and difficult. Halfway down Africa's west coast, the wind suddenly shifts. North of the equator, the wind blows from the northeast. South of the equator, it blows from the southeast. Ships sailing toward the Cape of Good Hope had a great deal of trouble fighting these southeastern winds.

Da Gama's plan was to sail southwest into the Atlantic Ocean to keep his ships' sails full as the northeast and southeast winds blew over their sides. When the ships sailed far enough, they would reach the zone of the westerlies, winds that constantly blow from west to east. Then, the fleet would turn to catch these winds, which would blow the ships past the bottom of Africa.

This would have worked, but da Gama turned his ships too soon. The fleet hit a region of dead calm, broken only by brief squalls. Most of the time, the ships sat still in an unmoving ocean. Eventually, food and water began to spoil. Disease spread through all four ships, killing many of the crew. It took three months before the ships were able to sail out of this area and into the Indian Ocean.

Bad luck stayed with da Gama throughout the rest of the journey. The three remaining ships were in desperate need of repair due to the damage that three months' exposure to the sun and still water had caused. (The supply ship had been stripped and burned according to da Gama's plan.) But Arab mer-

When da Gama successfully completed a voyage from Portugal to India in 1498, he overturned the longstanding belief that one could not sail around Africa to India.

POINTS OF SAILING

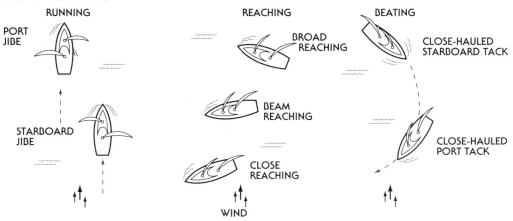

A ship sailing with the wind to its back is running. When running, a square sail is rigged to cut straight across the wind's path. On a small fore-and-aft-rigged ship, the sails stick straight out to one side. On a two-masted ship, one sail will stick out on each side of the boat. On a three-masted ship, the largest sail (usually the mainsail) will stick out to one side. The other two sails will hang over the opposite side to balance the larger sail. The sails on large fore-and-aft-rigged sailing ships are big enough that they do not need to stick over the side to catch the wind.

Ships do not always sail before the wind. Often, they have to sail at a diagonal to the direction the wind is blowing. This type of sailing is called reaching. There are three types of reaching. Broad reaching is sailing with the wind blowing over on the ship's rear quarters. In a broad reach, all sails stick out over the same side. They also point slightly towards the rear of the ship. Beam reaching is sailing with the wind blowing straight over the side of the ship. The sails point even more towards the rear of the ship in a beam reach, standing at roughly a 45-degree angle to the ship's centerline. Close reaching is

sailing nearly into the wind. In a close reach, the sails are nearly aligned with the keel of the ship. In this position, the sails begin acting like airplane wings, rather than as nets for the wind. While enough wind blows onto the rear of the sail to fill it out, most of the wind blows across the front of the sail. This action creates an area of low pressure in front of the sail. Just as a vacuum cleaner sucks up dirt, this low pressure area sucks the sail forward.

Sometimes, a ship must sail in the opposite direction that the wind is blowing. Since a ship cannot sail directly into the wind, the sailors must use a method of sailing called beating, or tacking. In beating, a ship zig-zags across the direction of the wind. The sails are set as close to the direction of the wind as possible, or close-hauled. The ship builds up speed, then turns directly into the wind. At that moment, the sails are shifted to hang over the opposite side of the ship. The ship's momentum and its rudder keep the ship turning until it points back across the wind. Once the ship has turned far enough, the wind catches the sails and the ship moves forward again. A ship cannot make this turn if it only has square sails, however.

chants who controlled trade along the eastern coast of Africa convinced the local African rulers to turn da Gama away when he tried to bring his ships in for repair. The Arabs did not want a competing power coming into their territory. Da Gama and his fleet had to sail to Malindi, a country on the "horn" of Africa's east coast, before they found a friendly harbor.

Da Gama finally reached India in early 1498. His fleet, with the aid of a guide from Malindi, crossed the Indian Ocean to reach the thriving trade center of Calicut. But the trade goods da Gama brought from Portugal turned out to be worthless to the Calicut merchants. Not wanting to send gold on this risky voyage, the king of Portugal had provided da Gama with a cargo of cloth and washbasins to trade. These items, however, were inferior to the products already available in India.

The best da Gama could do was buy a small cargo of pepper and other spices with a personal supply of gold he had carried with him. The journey back to Portugal was nearly a disaster as well. Da Gama had to abandon a second ship when disease killed most of its crew. By the time he returned to Portugal in 1499, fewer than 75 of the 150 men he had started with were still alive.

Despite da Gama's losses and bad luck, the king of Portugal considered the voyage a success. The small spice cargo da Gama brought back paid for the cost of the journey. More impor-

Da Gama negotiates a trade agreement in Calicut, India. This trade helped establish Portugal as an independent trading power.

tant, da Gama had proved that Portugal did not have to depend on Arab and Italian merchants. His country could now have its own place in world trade. In 1500, Portugal took the second step in that direction by sending to Calicut a fleet of thirteen ships loaded with gold to buy spices.

The Age of Discovery

The voyages Prince Henry inspired marked the start of a long period of exploration by European nations that bordered the sea. This period was called the age of discovery. It was part of the Renaissance, the period after the Middle Ages when European knowledge and culture blossomed. Many long-held ideas, such as the belief that one could not sail around Africa to India, were overturned.

But the voyages of the age of discovery would not have been possible without ships like the caravel and the carrack. These two ships—especially the carrack, with its combination of square and lateen sails—had the power and the range for deep-ocean travel. These ships were also able to carry the crew and the supplies needed for the long journeys the explorers faced. Once the new lands had been explored, merchants used these ships to establish and travel the trade routes.

Spain and the New World

The second nation to enter the age of discovery was Spain, Portugal's neighbor on the Iberian Peninsula. Spain, like Portugal, wanted an independent trade route to the spice lands. But its

Christopher Columbus intended to find a western route to the Far East. Instead he reached the New World and remained unaware of the significance of his discovery.

rulers were not able to use the same route as Portugal had. If Spain had begun to explore the same routes as Portugal, Spanish ships would have been in competition with the Portuguese, and this could have led to war.

In the 1480s, a Genoese sailor named Christopher Columbus approached the king and queen of Spain with a new plan for reaching the spice lands. Columbus believed India, China, and other Far

Columbus describes his voyages to the king and queen of Spain.

A wood engraving depicts Columbus's ships, the Santa Maria, Pinta, *and* Niña, *setting sail for the Far East.*

East countries lay on the western side of the Atlantic Ocean. Unfortunately, Columbus made a mistake in calculating the size of the earth when planning his voyage. Though Asia is actually more than ten thousand miles west of Spain, Columbus calculated the distance as only twenty-five hundred miles. Using these figures, Columbus believed he could sail west to China in less than two months.

Queen Isabella had faith in Columbus's plan. She gave the sailor enough money to assemble a fleet of three ships. Two of these ships—*Niña* and *Pinta*—were caravels. The third ship, the *Santa Maria*, was probably a carrack. (There is no accurate description of what the ships looked like. Columbus himself hated *Santa Maria*, his flagship. He felt it was too small and sailed poorly.) In September of 1492, the fleet sailed west from the port of Gomera in the Canary Islands.

One month later, Columbus and his crew landed on a small island. At the time, Columbus thought he had reached a group of islands lying far to the east of mainland China. Though he never knew it, he had, in fact, accomplished a more remarkable feat. He had landed on an island in the Bahamas, an island chain stretching southeast of Florida. Columbus had reached the New World. His landing was the first step in the eventual European exploitation and colonization of the American continents. But Columbus was unaware of the full extent of his discovery.

Vasco Nuñez de Balboa was the first to realize that Columbus had discovered a new continent twenty years before.

Portuguese explorer Ferdinand Magellan navigated a Spanish fleet to find a route past the American continents and on to the East Indies.

Balboa Discovers the Pacific

Other Spanish captains continued to explore the area now known as the Caribbean Sea for about twenty years before they realized that Columbus had discovered a whole new world. The explorer who first realized this fact was Vasco Nuñez de Balboa, who in 1513 crossed the Isthmus of Panama, which connects North and South America. On the western side of the isthmus, Balboa found something no one in Europe ever thought existed: a second ocean. Western scholars had thought the Atlantic Ocean was the only ocean in the world. In fact, it was common just to refer to it simply as "the ocean," or "the ocean sea." When sailors noticed how peaceful this new ocean was compared

to the stormy Atlantic, they named it the Pacific Ocean.

Yet these geographical breakthroughs did not bring Spain any closer to establishing a trade route to India. In 1519, a Portuguese navigator named Ferdinand Magellan took on the task. He commanded a five-ship Spanish fleet. Magellan proposed to find a route past the American continents to the East Indies. The king of Portugal had refused to pay for this expedition, but the king of Spain, Charles I, was more than happy to take advantage of Portugal's loss.

Loaded with trade goods, Magellan's ships sailed to the coast of Patagonia, a nation on the eastern coast of South America. There, the fleet waited out the winter. In the spring, Magellan's ships sailed south again. They soon found what appeared to be a passage through the tip of South America. This

Magellan and his crew discover a strait through South America that connects the Atlantic and Pacific oceans.

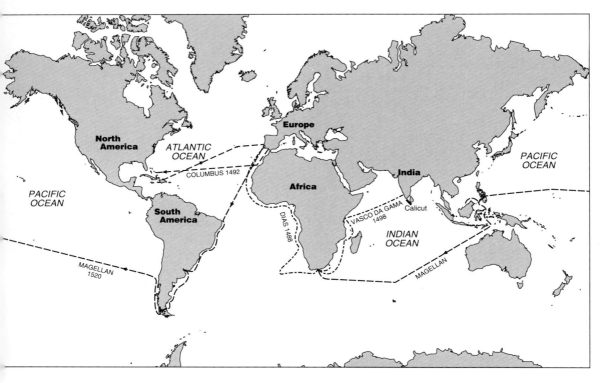

The lines above trace the historic voyages of European navigators Bartholmeu Dias, Vasco da Gama, Christopher Columbus, and Ferdinand Magellan.

passage turned out to be a treacherous, 310-mile strip of water connecting the Atlantic and Pacific oceans. It took the fleet thirty-eight hard days of sailing to reach the other side. From there, however, it was simply a matter of sailing east until the fleet reached the spice lands.

Results of the Age of Discovery

Having whole new lands and a new ocean to explore sent a shock wave across Europe. Nations like Great Britain and France took advantage of Columbus's discovery of the New World by establishing colonies. These colonies supplied the nations with food, timber for ships, and other products. France and Britain also hoped to discover gold or other treasures. Suddenly, people in Europe could buy cloth, spices, furniture, and other exotic goods that they had rarely been able to acquire. This newfound taste for imported goods spurred on the search for new and better trading opportunities. In turn, this search created the need for new and better ships.

Trading Beyond the Horizon

From the sixteenth to the nineteenth century, ships were developed to exploit the trade routes established during the age of discovery. Shipbuilders designed their vessels with two factors in mind. The main concern, of course, was designing the ships to hold as much cargo as possible. Whether taking gold from Mexico to Spain or carrying calico cloth from India to England, ships had to show a profit. Often, a single fleet's cargo meant wealth or poverty for a nation.

A trade ship also had to defend itself. Any trade ship, especially one that carried a particularly valuable cargo, was vulnerable to attack. Pirate ships and ships belonging to competing nations were constantly on the lookout for an easy target. Ships that sported a sturdy hull and a strong battery of cannons discouraged these attacks.

The Galleon and American Wealth

The best-known of the ships that incorporated these design elements was the galleon. The galleon was a heavier version of the carrack. Its hull stretched higher out of the water and was longer than the hull of the carrack. This extra room allowed the galleon to carry more cargo than two or three carracks. Its long decks were able to hold forty cannons.

The most striking feature of the galleon was its high, wide stern, which rose as much as thirty feet above the waves. Six to eight cannons could be mounted facing out of portholes cut in this larger stern. These cannons made the rear of the ship less vulnerable to attack. The new stern also served to dis-

The galleon, a trade ship, had a sturdy hull. Its high, wide stern held cannons to discourage attacks from pirate ships.

New sail combinations, including the addition of a sail at the top of each mast called a topgallant, increased the galleon's ability to sail in strong winds and carry heavy cargo and cannons.

play intricate carvings designed to impress foreigners with the wealth and sophistication of the galleon's country.

New sail combinations were created to give the galleons the power to move the heavy cannons and cargoes. Both the foremast and the mainmast were taller and carried larger sails. In addition to the mainsails and topsails, a third sail called the topgallant was rigged at the top of each mast. The mizzenmast was joined by a smaller bonaventure mizzen, increasing the galleon's ability to sail against the wind.

Spanish Treasure Fleets

Spain, in particular, used ships like these to aid in the exploitation of its new American lands. Spanish explorers had discovered large, easily mined deposits of silver in Mexico and had found gold mines in South America. The large

galleons, which had the firepower to defend themselves from attack, were perfect for transporting this wealth. Some of the galleons were used for hauling cargo, while others were used strictly to defend the fleet. Galleons formed great treasure fleets that sailed from the Americas to Spain each year. The Spanish treasury came to depend on these yearly shipments to sustain Spain's far-reaching kingdom. At times, Spain lost a fleet or a few of its ships to storms or pirates. These mishaps often made the difference between rich years and poor ones in Spain.

Spanish explorers also sailed west over the Pacific Ocean to the Philippines. There, they traded American silver for silk and other Asian products. Soon, galleons were making regular trading journeys across the Pacific.

To avoid conflicts over newly discovered countries and trade routes, Spain and Portugal decided to split the world between them. Portugal agreed to stay out of the New World, except for a part of Brazil that Portuguese sailors had already claimed. Spain, in turn, agreed not to use Portugal's trade route around Africa or to take over the Portuguese trading ports in Africa.

The other nations of Europe were furious at this decision. But for most of the sixteenth century, they were powerless to do much about it. Great Britain, Holland, and France did conduct explorations of North America during this time. For these voyages, they used their own version of the Spanish galleon. They also established colonies in modern-day New England and Canada. Spain took little notice of these journeys into its part of the world because there were no spices, gold, or silver in these areas. But Spain and Portugal kept strict control over their trade

The galleon's regular journeys across the Pacific facilitated trade between Europe and the Americas.

routes. It was not until the 1590s that other nations grew strong enough to challenge Spain and Portugal.

The Fluyt and the V.O.C.

Northern Europe had many problems after the year 1000. Great Britain, France, Holland, and other nations continually fought each other over land, trade, and which person should succeed the throne when a king died. Diseases like the black plague killed hundreds of thousands of people. Those who survived had much to rebuild. Progress in shipping did not stop, however. People still needed things that only ships could provide. And while Spain and Portugal set about conquering the New World, other countries quietly began dominating the old one.

Holland, which is today called the Netherlands, was the first country to develop trading fleets to compete with the Iberian Peninsula. Once a province of Spain, Holland provided ports that gave Spain both military and economic dominance from the Iberian Peninsula to Denmark. Eventually, the Dutch got tired of being a conquered nation. In 1568, Holland began to rebel. Spain eventually pulled out of Holland after thirty-seven years of intermittent fighting and a thirty-nine-year truce. With their freedom restored, the Dutch began to establish themselves as independent seafarers. They took over trade in the Baltic Sea. Dutch ships carried cargoes of imported spices from Portugal to northern Europe. By the late sixteenth century, Holland was the Western world's major trading power.

The Dutch dominated this trade because they charged less to transport their goods. They were able to offer inexpensive service because they had designed better ships. In other countries, ships were designed much like the Spanish galleons. They were built to be able to defend themselves as well as to carry cargo. They were armored with heavier planking that could stand up to cannon fire. They also had at least one row of cannons on each side.

The drawback to all this protection was that the ships were harder to handle. The extra weight of the planking and cannons reduced a ship's speed and maneuverability. To maneuver the ships, crews were large, usually composed of at least thirty seamen. Dutch ships were lighter and easier to maneuver. A system of ropes and pulleys let a handful of men raise or lower sail. A Dutch ship carried more cargo than any other ship on the seas.

The most advanced example of the Dutch ship was the *fluyt*, or flyboat. It was produced in 1595 as a large-capacity trade vessel for use in the Baltic Sea and North Sea. The fluyt was about as wide as a galleon, but it was longer than any other ship afloat. As a result, it had more cargo space than either the carrack or the galleon.

Though lighter than a galleon, the fluyt was not fast. It was designed for slow, safe, reliable shipping. Dutch shipowners felt that merchants would wait for their goods if they did not have to pay much to ship them. The ship-owners turned out to be right. By the middle of the seventeenth century, the fluyt was the general cargo ship of Holland, Great Britain, France, and Germany. Dutch merchants even acted as middlemen for trade between France and Great Britain and their North American colonies.

In the sixteenth century the Dutch dominated trade in the Western world by utilizing ships that could carry more cargo than those of their competitors.

A Dutch trading fleet carries merchants and their goods to their trade destination.

The money the Dutch merchants earned went into building ships that could make the voyage to India. The first trading voyage from Holland to the Indies took place in 1595. In 1602, a group of merchants founded the Dutch East India Company to agree not to compete with each other, which would drive shipping costs too low. The V.O.C. (the company's Dutch initials) made Holland the century's leading merchant power.

Major Shipping Powers on the Decline

By 1602, the Portuguese controlled shipping routes to India from fortresses in the Indian Ocean. To counter Portugal's trading power, the V.O.C. saturated the trading lanes with its own merchant ships and warships. By the 1620s, its ships outnumbered the Portuguese two to one. The company blockaded Portugal's fortresses and trading ports. It also attacked and captured Portuguese ships of all types. By the middle of the century, Portugal had been eliminated as the controlling power in the Far East.

Spain's fall was not far behind. Holland, France, and Great Britain had be-

come more aggressive in settling the New World. They began harassing Spanish ships, especially the treasure fleets that carried Spain's silver and gold. Then two disasters struck Spain within three years of each other. In 1625, Spain's richest silver mines stopped producing. The great veins of metal had been used up. Spain had to rely even more upon its sources in South America. Then, in 1628, a fleet of Dutch vessels captured Spain's entire silver fleet as it was sailing home. This was the first of many such seizures of Spanish ships. To make matters worse, ships from Holland, Great Britain, and France captured Spanish ports throughout the Caribbean Sea. By 1660, Spain had lost control of its empire.

Tea Trade and the Indiaman

The elimination of Spain and Portugal as merchant powers left the world open to the other European nations. France colonized the Caribbean and parts of northern South America. Holland established plantations and trading settlements in the East Indies spice lands.

Great Britain also tried to break into the spice trade. In fact, Queen

Elizabeth I had granted a charter forming a British East India Company two years before the V.O.C. But conflicts with Holland after 1620 convinced Great Britain to stay out of Indonesia. By this time, however, spices were not vital to Europe any more because Europeans no longer had to worry about masking the flavor of rancid meat. Farmers had discovered root crops that could be stored and used to feed animal herds in the winter.

The Orient, however, had more to offer than spices. Muslin and calico fabrics were becoming popular items in Europe. And in 1684, Emperor K'anghsi opened the Chinese tea market to foreigners. These three products became the staples of British trade in the Far East. They also led to Great Britain's rule of India and involvement in the politics of China.

Trade Prompts Change

Once again, trade prompted a change in ship design. This time, shipbuilders did not change the size of the ship so much as its outward appearance. The Indiaman, as the ship was called, was an exercise in deception. Most of its space was set aside for cargo. Little room was left for weaponry. To keep pirates and enemy ships away, the Indiaman was painted and rigged to look like a warship.

Fake gun ports were cut or painted along the sides of the Indiaman. The effect was to give the ship the impression of having thirty or forty guns. The sails and shape of the upper deck mimicked those of a fighting ship. The ship's officers even dressed like their counterparts in the Royal Navy.

All of these deceptions were designed to fool an enemy ship. A seaman looking through a telescope would see what appeared to be a fully armed warrior patrolling the trading lanes. Shipbuilders and shipowners hoped the disguise would be enough to scare off potential raiders. From the success these ships had in delivering their cargoes on time, it seemed the ruse was a success.

The resemblance to a warship stopped below the main deck. The Indiaman was designed as much for passenger travel as it was for cargo hauling. The cabins below deck were set up for the comfort of their occupants. And while the Indiaman could sail fast when needed, it usually sailed at a reasonably

Queen Elizabeth I approved a British East India Company, but Great Britain decided not to trade in Indonesia because of conflicts with Holland's V.O.C.

The Indiaman carried passengers and cargo but was rigged to look like a warship. The disguise was successful, and the ships delivered their cargo without fear of attack.

slow speed. An average trip from Canton to England, for example, took about five months.

By the time the Indiaman was built, the principles of rigging and hull design had been worked out. Aside from warships, there were no great leaps in ship development from the seventeenth to the nineteenth century. That does not mean there were no changes in ship design. Ships of many shapes and sizes were produced during these two hundred years or so. There were barks, barkentines, schooners, and sloops, to name a few. Colonists in the New World came up with variations of the European ships. Some of the colonies fought for and won their independence using these ships. Afterward, they supported themselves with their own merchant ships.

Nonetheless, these ships were simply alterations on the designs of the carrack, the galleon, and the fluyt. No radical shift in ship design appeared until the 1820s.

Clippers and the End of Sail Power

The American Revolution was only one of two wars the United States fought with Great Britain. In the War of 1812, the United States reaffirmed the freedom it had won. It also affirmed the right of U.S. merchants to trade in ports of their choosing.

Part of the reason for the War of 1812 was British interference with American shipping. British ships had

Great Britain's interference with trade between America and France was one cause of the War of 1812.

JAMES COOK

A second age of discovery took place beginning in the late seventeenth century. This time, nations were not searching for trade routes. Instead, they were looking for a legendary continent in the South Pacific Ocean. This continent was called Terra Australis, the "southern land."

Ships from many Western nations—including Great Britain, Spain, and France—searched for this mythical land. During this time, people believed that the universe was ruled by a system of balancing forces. According to the maps of the time, South America and Africa did not have enough land to balance out Europe and Asia. Therefore, scholars thought, there must be a continent in the South Pacific.

The search continued well into the eighteenth century. By far the greatest of the mariners who sought the southern continent was an Englishman named James Cook. Cook was known as the best navigator and one of the best captains of his time. He was also known for his high principles of professionalism and duty. Cook had enlisted in the Royal Navy before the start of a major war between the great powers of Europe. This was a very unusual move. Cook had been the first mate, which is second in command, of a coal ship. Nevertheless, he wanted to serve his country during the coming conflict. He was willing to go to work as an ordinary seaman to do so.

Cook survived the war, which lasted from 1756 to 1763. His skill and personality had raised him from his position as seaman to an officer. Soon, Cook was in command of his own ship.

HMS *Endeavour* originally was to have been a private coal ship. But the Royal Navy needed a ship that could carry enough crew and supplies for an extended voyage in the Pacific Ocean. The large cargo holds and sturdy construction of this ship were just what was needed. The navy bought the small, tubby ship and refitted it as a vessel of exploration.

Endeavour was an unqualified success. Cook was pleased with the construction of the little ship. He was also pleased with its reliability and ease of handling. When his first voyage was over, Cook requested to be assigned only to ships like *Endeavour*.

Cook made three voyages in the South and North Pacific from 1768 to 1779. Among the lands he charted were

Englishman James Cook, an explorer during the second age of discovery, was known as the best navigator of his time. He charted islands in the South and North Pacific.

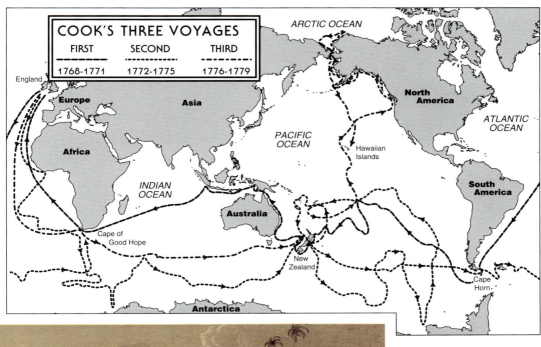

COOK'S THREE VOYAGES

FIRST	SECOND	THIRD
1768-1771	1772-1775	1776-1779

A map displays the three voyages of Captain Cook (above). Natives greet Cook and his crew as they land in Hawaii.

Tahiti, New Zealand, the Hawaiian Islands, the Bering Strait near Alaska, and Vancouver Island to the west of British Columbia. Sadly, Cook did not live to see the end of his third voyage. In 1779, he was killed by a group of Hawaiian Islanders during a dispute over his crew's behavior on shore.

The second age of discovery lasted until nearly the end of the eighteenth century. When it was over, there were virtually no uncharted islands left in the Pacific Ocean. Better still, a small continent had been found lying to the southeast of China. This continent was given the name of the southern land everyone had been searching for and was called Australia.

An American naval ship battles with a British ship during the War of 1812. At the end of the war, Great Britain agreed to respect America's trading rights.

prevented American merchants from delivering goods to France during a war between the two European countries. Worse, members of the Royal Navy would board American merchant vessels and kidnap crew members. These Americans would then be enlisted against their will as sailors in the Royal Navy. At the end of the war, Britain agreed to stop this practice and to respect U.S. trading rights.

Merely having the right to trade did not mean American merchants would be successful, however. Like any other business people, they had to compete with well-established and experienced rivals. Great Britain, France, and Holland were still the major sea traders of the world. Breaking into international markets was a hard job. U.S. merchants needed ships that would give them an edge over their competition. And they needed to ship products they knew would sell.

Fortunately, the slow progression of ship design gave the merchants the edge they needed. Shipbuilders in Maryland had come up with a very fast though fairly small type of schooner. From the start, this ship had been designed for speed. Its hull was sharp and narrow, reaching its widest point aft of

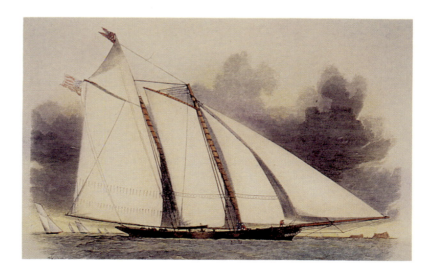

Built for speed, the schooner helped U.S. merchants compete in international trade.

its midsection. Combined with a forward-slanting bow, this design let the ship slice through the waves.

At the back, the hull ended in a rearward slant that stuck out over the rudder. This feature kept the stern from building up suction and slowing the ship down as it was pulled along over the sea. The ship also had masts almost as tall as the keel was long. These masts were literally masked by square and lateen sails. The goal was to have the ship capture every scrap of wind possible, to get as much speed out of every breeze. Since it was designed to clip short the time needed to make certain scheduled crossings, these ships became known as clippers.

Clipper owners only needed two things: a cargo of goods and a market to carry them to. Fortunately, something happened that fulfilled both needs almost overnight. In 1848, a California miller named John Sutter found gold in the stream running past his property. This find marked the beginning of the great California gold rush. More than eighty thousand prospectors rushed to California in 1849. But they arrived with few provisions, which started a second rush. This time, it was a rush by merchants to open stores and stock supplies to sell to the miners.

The new market that opened up seemed tailor-made for the clipper owners. Here was a booming society that desperately needed the fast delivery of essential goods. That was the task the clipper had been built for. At the time, no railroad service to the western United States existed. The transcontinental railroad would not be built until the 1860s. Transporting cargo in wagons could take up to six months. Clip-

The clipper quickly transported goods to the settlers of the California gold rush.

pers, on the other hand, could sail around South America from New England in as little as three months. Considering the profit they could make on their goods, merchants did not mind paying for the cost of the rapid delivery.

For people in the early 1800s, clippers seemed like the ships of the future. A national mania for news about these fast ships soon sprang into being. The general public began following the clippers' trips like modern football fans track their favorite teams.

In Great Britain, tea merchants had been looking for a faster way to carry tea from China. Until the 1840s, they had relied on the old Indiaman, which usually took five months to make the trip. The British tea merchants soon adopted the clipper design and cut the amount of time it took to complete the trip to China from five to three months.

To the captains of these vessels, the clipper seemed as fast as the wind itself. Some clippers posted speeds of three hundred nautical miles or more in a single day. Indeed, a clipper's speed was limited only by how fast the wind blew and how much sail was spread out to catch it.

The clippers were not perfect, however. The clipper ship was a thoroughbred. It had been crafted specifically for the task of high-speed sailing. It did not have a great deal of cargo space but could carry small, easily stowed loads of goods. Like thoroughbreds of the animal world, clippers were fast, but more prone to mishaps. Their lighter framework resulted in broken spars and masts, snapped riggings, and other disasters.

Deaths among the clipper crews were high as well. In some cases, half a clipper's crew was composed of men who knew nothing of shipboard life but had been impressed into service. Their problems were often compounded by hard-driving captains who cared more for their schedule than for human life.

California clippers stop at their dock in the East before sailing around South America back to California.

Although the fastest cargo ship of its day, the clipper had its drawbacks. Its lighter framework made it susceptible to broken spars and masts. The clipper ship Cutty Sark *is pictured here.*

Sailors who were washed or knocked overboard were given up for lost so that the ship would not lose time on its run. Frequently, a crew's anger flared into an attempt to kill the captain and the clipper's officers.

Many crews who did not attempt a revolt against the captain, called mutiny, would desert the ship once it reached its destination. During the gold rush, many ships had to be abandoned in San Francisco Bay when their crews headed for the goldfields. Veteran seamen who might have held these crews together were rarely part of a clipper's crew. They knew better than to ship out on these mutiny-plagued deathtraps.

The general public did not see or hear much of this side of clipper life. They preferred to be enchanted by the clipper's speed and beauty. Some people think the clippers were the greatest accomplishment in the history of sailing. Sadly, they came at the end of the period of dominance of the high seas by sailing ships. By the end of the 1870s, clipper ships had all but disappeared from the mainstream of world trade, following a gradual decline of wooden-hulled sailing ships that took place throughout the nineteenth century. In their place came a new type of ship that was able to sail regardless of where or when the winds blew.

CHAPTER 4

A New Form of Power

By the 1830s, sailing ships were as efficient as they were ever going to be. The clippers traveled as fast as a sailing ship could possibly go. But they could not carry more cargo than the slower trading ships.

Despite the advances in sailing, one problem still existed. A sailing ship could only go where and when the wind allowed. If the wind did not blow, the ship could not move. As a result, ship travel remained a slow, uncertain business. In addition to the vagaries of the wind, ship travel was uncertain because captains did not sail until their hold was full. This meant that passenger travel and mail delivery were undependable.

In an attempt to compete with larger shipping companies and offer an alternative to uncertain departure dates, an American shipping company called the Black Ball Line went into business with the first regular, sched-uled departures of mail and passenger ships to England in 1828. These ships were called packets. Scheduled departures meant that people could be sure of leaving at a certain time.

The day of arrival, however, still depended upon the weather. No company could schedule that. Most of the time, the Black Ball packets arrived within twenty days of their departure. But the journey was a cramped one for all but the richest passengers. What shipowners and customers alike needed was a big ship that could overcome the uncertainty of wind power.

Steam Power Goes to Sea

In 1720, a British blacksmith named Thomas Newcomen began experimenting with steam power, basing his work on the ideas of a scientist named Denis

Passengers on a packet could be assured of a scheduled departure date. Their arrival day, however, depended on the weather.

44 ■ SHIPS

Denis Papin theorized that a steam engine could run on atmospheric pressure.

Papin. Papin, who had invented the first pressure cooker, had also written a theory of how to build a practical steam engine. Papin theorized that a piston-and-cylinder pump could be powered by using the pressure of the atmosphere. The space between the piston head and the inside of the cylinder could be filled with steam, then rapidly cooled. As the steam cooled, it would form a vacuum in the cylinder. Atmospheric pressure would push the piston toward the top of the cylinder.

Newcomen believed he could make an engine very much like the one Papin described and make money with it. Newcomen worked on his engine for ten years before he got it to work. When it was finished, it looked pretty much like the machine Papin had described. A piston was hung upside down in the cylinder. A counterweight was attached to the piston to raise it off the cylinder's floor. At the same time, steam was piped into the cylinder through a small pipe.

Once the cylinder was full, a valve shot a jet of cold water into the cylinder. The water helped the steam condense and draw the piston back down. A system of ropes and pulleys connected the steam and water valves to the post that held the piston and counterweight so that the engine was able to open these valves by itself.

Newcomen thought his engine could be used for water travel. He built a riverboat and hooked his engine to a series of twelve paddles mounted on a moving iron framework over the boat. Newcomen wanted the engine to move six paddles on each side of the boat. He engineered the paddles so that three of them would be stroking the water on each side all the time. Newcomen hoped the alternating stroke of the paddles would move the boat smoothly through the water. Unfortunately, the idea failed. The paddles were not powerful enough to move the boat against the river's current. This failure effectively ended Newcomen's experiments with steam-powered water travel.

Improving Newcomen's Design

In 1764, an engineer named James Watt found a way to improve Newcomen's design. Watt realized that because the steam had to raise the weighted bar that, in turn, raised the piston, the Newcomen engine was wasting a good deal of the steam's energy. Watt improved upon Newcomen's design by building a water-cooled condensing unit separate from the cylinder. He also added a second steam pipe to the top of the cylinder. That way, steam could push against both sides of the piston. Valves at both

EARLY STEAM ENGINES

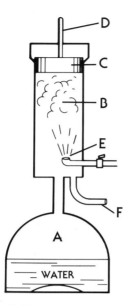

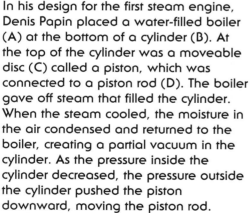

PAPIN & NEWCOMEN

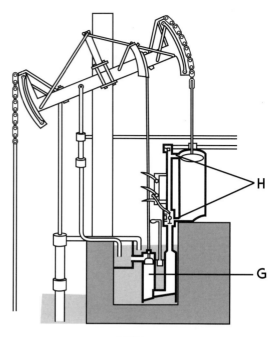

WATT

In his design for the first steam engine, Denis Papin placed a water-filled boiler (A) at the bottom of a cylinder (B). At the top of the cylinder was a moveable disc (C) called a piston, which was connected to a piston rod (D). The boiler gave off steam that filled the cylinder. When the steam cooled, the moisture in the air condensed and returned to the boiler, creating a partial vacuum in the cylinder. As the pressure inside the cylinder decreased, the pressure outside the cylinder pushed the piston downward, moving the piston rod.

Papin's engine was powerful, but slow. It took a long time for the steam in the cylinder to condense and draw the piston down. Thomas Newcomen increased the speed of the engine by adding a condensing jet (E) that sprayed cold water into the cylinder. The cold water caused the steam to condense quickly, increasing the speed of the piston. Newcomen also added an eduction pipe (F), so the water from the condensing jet would drain out of the chamber without cooling the water in the boiler.

James Watt realized that Newcomen's design wasted much of the steam's energy, since it condensed upon contact with cool air already in the cylinder. To prevent this loss of power, Watt's engine had a separate condensing chamber (G) where the steam was cooled by a cold water jet. Watt also added a second steam pipe (H) to the cylinder, allowing steam to be admitted on both sides of the piston. With steam pushing the piston in both directions, the engine became more efficient.

James Watt improved Newcomen's steam engine design, making it both more efficient and powerful.

had a tendency to explode if the steam pressure got even a little bit too high and it still burned a lot of fuel. But for its time, it was a technological marvel. It held the promise of providing constant power in exchange for little maintenance. For inventive shipbuilders, Watt's engine was a promising new device.

Fitch Brings Steam Power to Ships

John Fitch was such an inventor. The American boat builder and engineer dreamed of sailing along the nation's rivers using steam power. He envisioned a craft having a wheel made up of flat boards that would, like a series of paddles, push the boat through the water. This arrangement would imitate the action of a human rower, but at a faster, more constant rate. Fitch knew his design would give enough power to move the boat—all the engine had to do was turn a wheel. By 1786, Fitch had succeeded in building a side-wheeled boat that could carry two men upstream along any river in New England.

ends of the cylinder opened to let out old steam as the piston was pushed in the opposite direction. As the piston moved, it pushed the old steam off to the condenser. This design change made Watt's engine both more powerful and more fuel-efficient than Newcomen's.

Even after Watt's alterations, the steam engine was not perfect. Its boiler

John Fitch's steamboat used steam power to push a wheel which could propel the boat upstream. It was not, however, a commercial success.

Four years later, Fitch followed up on this success with a larger freight and passenger boat. This vessel had a single paddle wheel at the stern. It was faster than Fitch's first craft and had a top speed of eight miles per hour. Fitch designed his stern-wheeler for regular service on the Delaware River. He hoped to run a commuter service between Philadelphia, Pennsylvania, and Trenton, New Jersey. Unfortunately, his vision turned out to be a commercial failure. It may have been that people distrusted this newfangled way of traveling. They may have feared a midstream boiler explosion. Or they might have felt that the paddleboat was too slow. Horse-drawn coaches had an average speed of roughly ten miles per hour. Whatever the reason, Fitch went out of business in 1791.

Robert Fulton Improves Fitch's Design

The idea of steam-powered sailing had not died, however. In the first decade of the nineteenth century, another American engineer took up the challenge. Robert Fulton had studied the use of steam power during a twenty-year sojourn to Europe. Fulton also learned about shipbuilding while working for the French government on a very early version of the submarine. At that time, Europe was more advanced than the United States in the use of steam power. People who wanted to learn about this technology often went overseas to study.

During his studies, Fulton began building steam-powered machinery. In fact, he was well known for inventing, among other things, a steam-powered digging machine. In 1805, he moved to New York City and began working on a way to successfully combine steam power with ship travel.

When Fulton started building his steamboat, the *Clermont*, people poked fun at what they were sure would be another madman's failure. "Fulton's folly" they called the 150-foot, side-wheel steamboat.

On September 4, 1807, Fulton's ship, *Clermont*, sailed from New York City to Albany along the Hudson River. The fact that it made the long journey (more than three times the distance Fitch's ship traveled) without mishap proved steam power's reliability. People were soon using Fulton's steamship instead of horse-drawn carriages. Fulton continued building and promoting steamships for use on the nation's rivers. By the time of his death in 1815, seventeen paddle wheelers were making regular trips along the Hudson and Mississippi rivers.

The success of "Fulton's folly" was the break the sea ship owners were look-

Robert Fulton used his knowledge of steam power to successfully design and build a 150-foot steamboat.

Fulton's steamboat, the Clermont, *sailed from New York City to Albany, proving the worth of steam power.*

ing for. If this new technology could be adapted for sea use, they could begin offering regular service between the continents. One group of shipowners decided to make use of the paddle wheel concept as soon as possible. They built a sailing ship that also had a collapsible steam-driven paddle wheel for when the wind was poor.

The ship they built was called the *Savannah*. It was largely a failure. Shipbuilders had underestimated the differences between ocean and river sailing. The paddle wheels broke easily in the rough sea waves. The hull itself was too weak to handle the stress of the ninety-horsepower engine. Because *Savannah* had a wooden skeleton and wooden hull planks, the engine could only be run at a fraction of its speed or the vibrations would rip the ship apart.

Despite the *Savannah*'s failure, many shipbuilders knew that steam power was the way of the future. At the forefront of these optimists were the shipowners of Great Britain.

The Voyages of the *Great Western*

Isambard Kingdon Brunel was the best railroad design engineer Britain's Great Western Railroad had seen. Brunel, the son of a French construction engineer, was acknowledged as one of the century's most inventive geniuses. He was also a champion of the idea of international steam travel.

In the 1830s, the Great Western Railroad Company was building a rail line from London to the seaport of Bristol on England's western coast. Brunel, however, had a vision of continuing the line across the Atlantic to New York City via ship. He imagined a large steamship picking up passengers and freight for a transatlantic cruise. The image of such a ship (and of the profits it would bring in) convinced the railroad's board of directors to support Brunel's plan.

Brunel went to work, designing the steamship and supervising its construction. He decided to make the ship a wooden-hulled paddle wheeler. To keep the hull from shaking apart, Brunel made it heavy and durable. He also reinforced the hull with diagonal iron braces. By 1838, the steamship *Great Western* was ready to sail. In addition to its paddle wheels, *Great Western* carried a full set of sails. These sails served to reassure sailors and passengers who did not trust the ship's engines to last for the entire trip.

Their worries proved groundless as the ship steamed steadily westward with-

Isambard Kingdon Brunel designed a steamship that carried passengers and cargo across the Atlantic from England to New York.

ropean shipbuilders began making ships with iron hull plates. By the late 1830s, small iron-hulled paddle wheelers were crossing the English Channel.

Brunel sailed on one of these steamers in October 1838, six months after *Great Western*'s maiden voyage. He was extremely impressed by the stability and strength of the iron hull. He also realized that an iron hull could be made much larger than one made of wood. A larger hull meant more room for cargo and for paying passengers.

A New Propeller

After construction began on the *Great Britain*, Brunel made an even more radical decision. He wanted to abandon the paddle wheel design. Paddle wheels were known to be inefficient because only part of the wheel's bottom half projected into the water. If the ship rolled or pitched even slightly, the wheel could lift totally out of the sea, making it useless. This was another reason early steamships carried sails. Brunel had seen ships with propulsion devices based on a water pump developed by the Greek inventor Archimedes, and he wanted his new ship to sport one. Archimedes' pump was a large, open-ended screw that stuck into a pond or a river. This screw—really a thin wooden plank coiled around a pole—rested in a rounded trough. When someone turned the screw, water became trapped between the coils of the plank. The coils then lifted the water to the top of the trough.

Shipbuilders thought that Archimedes' pump could be adapted for use as a ship's propeller. The first such propellers were long, hollow pipes wound

out having to stop for repairs. *Great Western*'s maiden voyage took only sixteen days. This time competed well with that of the sailing packets, which had to have perfect sailing conditions to make the trip as quickly. Naturally, the triumphant *Great Western* convinced many people to switch over from the Black Ball Line and other packet companies.

Buoyed by this success, the railroad directors decided to build a second, even larger ship, called the *Great Britain*. Brunel made a series of radical changes in the new ship's design. One of the main changes was that a new material was used to construct the ship. By the 1800s, British industrialists had figured out a way of melting and treating iron so that it could be formed into thin plates. These plates could be easily attached to an iron framework using iron rivets. Euwith metal coils instead of wooden ones. This design worked, but the experimental ships that used it went slowly.

Then, in 1784, a British inventor named Joseph Bramah had an idea. He saw that the problem with the Archimedes-type propeller was that the coils "tunneled" through too little water at a time. Bramah wanted to improve the design to move large amounts of water in a short space.

Bramah's design duplicated the design of a windmill—a wheel surrounded by a number of wide metal vanes. These vanes bit into the water, pushing a large amount of water to the rear of the ship. Because the propeller had the effect of screwing itself through the water, it became known as the screw propeller.

Two shipbuilders, England's Francis Smith and America's John Ericsson, received separate patents for ships using versions of Bramah's device. Smith finished building his ship before Ericsson did, taking the credit for launching the world's first screw-driven steamship. The ship was named, in tribute to the inventory of the water screw, the *Archimedes*.

Brunel saw a demonstration of *Archimedes* soon after construction began on *Great Britain*. The efficiency of the new screw propeller convinced Brunel to install a similar device on his new ship. Brunel knew the propeller would move his ship more efficiently than paddle wheels could.

Screw propellers had an added benefit. Paddle wheels were vulnerable to the elements. So steamships had large boxes covering the above-water portion of each wheel. Unfortunately, these boxes acted as gigantic air brakes when the ship steamed into the wind. Switching to propellers eliminated this wind resistance.

The First Modern Ship

In virtually all respects, *Great Britain* was the first truly modern ship. The only holdover from the old wooden ships was the addition of six masts to its top deck, in case the engines failed. Its new propellers featured six blades, the same design used for modern oil tankers. And its rudder was designed so the

The Great Britain *was the first modern ship. It ran on screw propellers instead of paddle wheels, and was the largest ship in the world in 1845.*

THE ARCHIMEDEAN SCREW

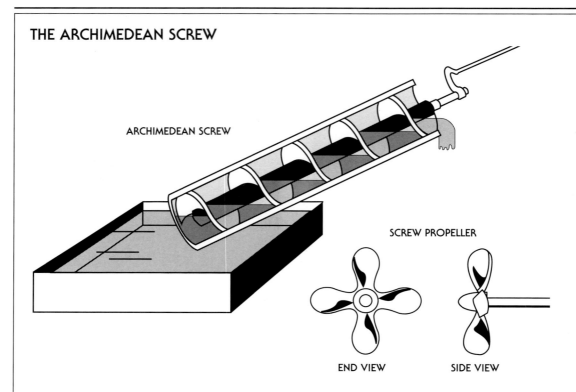

ARCHIMEDEAN SCREW

SCREW PROPELLER

END VIEW   SIDE VIEW

Searching for an efficient way of propelling a ship through the water, nineteenth-century shipbuilders turned to a device built more than two thousand years before by the Greek mathematician and engineer, Archimedes. Born in Sicily about 287 B.C., Archimedes invented a water pump that was used to drain water from the holds of ships and to irrigate crops along the Nile River in Egypt. The Archimedean screw consists of a flat plane of metal or other material wrapped in a spiral around a large rod. The screw rests inside a tube or in a trough. One end of the device is submerged in water, while the other end is placed above a tank or an irrigation ditch. As the screw turns, it in effect slices the water into small blocks and forces them to the top of the pump.

Beginning in the seventeenth century, inventors and shipbuilders proposed using Archimedean-type screws for ship propulsion. They believed an Archimedean screw attached to the bottom of a ship would bore its way through the water, pulling the ship along with it. Some small ships were built using this type of propulsion device, but they were very slow.

In the 1780s, Joseph Bramah realized that the force generated by the Archimedean screw was too small to propel a ship. However, Bramah believed that a smaller screw, one designed like a windmill, could generate more power by moving a small mass of water more efficiently. He built a large wheel with curved vanes and placed it beneath the ship. Like the Archimedean screw, Bramah's propeller bored through the water, forcing a large amount of water to the rear of the ship. This device became known as the screw propeller.

tiller post, which helps sailors turn the rudder, passed through the rudder's center of gravity. This balanced rudder was easier to turn as well as less likely to fall off or break down.

When it was finished in 1845, *Great Britain* was the largest ship in the world. It measured 322 feet long by 50.5 feet at its widest point. The distance between the keel and the top deck was roughly 50 feet. Inside, the ship featured more than 130 passenger cabins. Its main dining room was more than 100 feet long. The ship was also one of the sturdiest vessels afloat. In fact, *Great Britain* became famous for running aground off the Irish coast during its fifth voyage across the Atlantic Ocean and sustaining little damage.

Steam Conquers Sail

Despite the success of ships such as *Great Britain*, steam power was slow to establish itself in world shipping. Because they were more complicated and required an engine, steamships were expensive to build. It cost far more to build even a small steamship than it did to build a sailing packet. Ship losses were common, and few people wished to risk losing such a costly vessel.

Another problem was that, despite the physical comfort they offered, early steamships were smoky, smelly, noisy contraptions. The nautical piston-driven steam engines used a lot of coal to heat water into steam. Often, a ship would use all of its fuel supply and resort to sail power to complete a journey. Paddle wheelers especially were notorious coal wasters. Americans began calling these ships "British smoke boxes."

Advances in ship engine design gradually eliminated the pollution problem. One of the most important developments was the introduction of the compression steam engine. This engine was a more advanced version of James Watt's. Watt's engine used only the steam it generated to move the piston one time. This method used a lot of fuel to produce a relatively small reaction. The compression engine, however, passes the steam from one cylinder to another. Finally, the steam becomes too cold to exert any more pressure. It is

The Great Britain *was large and sturdy. It measured 322 feet long by 50.5 feet at its widest point.*

DIESEL POWER

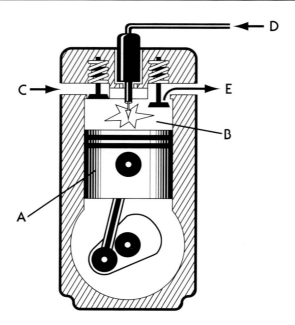

As sailing ships disappeared from the world's shipping lanes, shipowners began demanding engines that were more powerful and more efficient. Between 1880 and today, a number of innovative designs were developed or adapted for use aboard the world's trade, passenger, and fighting ships. These developments included the diesel engine.

The diesel engine was invented in 1897 by a German engineer, Rudolf Diesel. Like the steam engine, the diesel engine works by moving a piston (A) up and down inside a cylinder (B).

As the piston moves down, it draws in air through the intake valve (C). When the intake valve closes, the piston moves up, compressing the air in the closed chamber. As the air is compressed, it heats up. At the moment of greatest compression and heat, a fuel injector (D) sprays a fine mist of heating oil into the cylinder. The superheated air ignites the fuel, creating an explosion inside the cylinder. The expanding gases from this explosion push the piston downward with tremendous force. The exhaust valve (E) opens, allowing the gases to escape from the chamber.

Because fuel ignites inside the engine, the diesel is known as an internal combustion engine.

then sent to the condenser to start the cycle over again. The newer engines also cut down on the amount of coal the ships had to consume.

The steamship had other advantages that made people prefer it to sailing ships. Steamships were faster than even the swiftest clipper ship. As soon as shipbuilders began building steel hulls in the 1850s, steamships became both stronger and lighter than ships built with iron. By the 1880s, few ships were being built with iron.

As steamship rates became less ex-

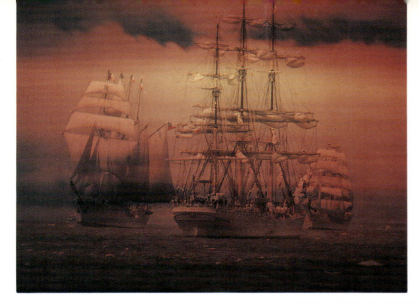

The windjammer, a huge sailing ship, was a last attempt to compete with steam power.

pensive, merchants and passengers began to abandon wind-driven vessels. By the end of the nineteenth century, steamships carried most of the world's trade goods. Only a handful of ships kept on sailing with the trade winds and then only to carry goods to out-of-the-way locations like Australia or some ports in South America.

Windjammers: Sailing's Last Gasp

A few shipowners maintained their faith in sail power. In the late 1800s, a new sailing ship was designed to compete with the rapidly expanding steamship trade. The ship looked like a huge iron- or steel-hulled clipper. It carried large fore-and-aft sails on up to seven tall masts. These sails were rigged with wire lines on steel booms, movable poles across the mast that hold the sail in place. They were so heavy that the crew could raise them only by using small, powerful engines called donkey engines.

This ship was called the windjammer. It was a last attempt to compete with steamships. Unfortunately for sup-

porters of the windjammer, steamships were able to travel faster with more cargo than the huge sailing ships could carry. Windjammers enjoyed a short, intense period of competition before dying out. A few were purchased by naval academies or other institutions as training ships. The rest were either sold as scrap or left to rust away in ports around the world.

Revolutions in Trade and Travel

The advent of mechanically powered ships revolutionized trade and passenger travel. Cargo ships running on steam or diesel fuel drastically cut the time it took to transport food and other merchandise. More rapid contact between countries was possible. Other mechanically powered ships were built to cater to business travelers and tourists.

Twentieth-Century Cargo Ships

Up until the late 1950s, cargo ships looked and were loaded much like the early sailing ships. Cases of goods were stacked onto pallets or bundled up in large nets. The cargo was then hoisted by crane into the ship's storage hold. Smaller loads were carried on board by hand.

Inside the ship, the goods were stowed wherever they would fit. Loading cargo was a delicate task. The captain or cargo officer had to be careful not to place the bulk of the cargo too far to one side. That would make the ship lean, or list, to that side. Listing made steering the ship much more difficult. It also increased the risk that the ship would capsize in rough seas.

Handling cargo this way took a lot of time. Ships often had to stay in port for weeks unloading and loading their goods. Shipping companies decided that what they needed was an easier, more standardized way to load cargo.

The problem with general cargo ships was that no one could say what type of cargo would be going out on a particular voyage. Oil tankers, grain ships, and timber ships did not have these problems. They were designed to haul only one type of cargo. The captain of a general merchant freighter, on the other hand, could be faced with anything from televisions to teddy bears. Odd-shaped items were another problem.

Shipbuilders who worked for freighter companies figured out a way to overcome all these problems in one shot. Why not carry a cargo load in standard units? If all merchandise were packed in a standard-size metal container, it would be easier to store on board the ship.

The world's shipping companies designed two sizes of container. One size was forty feet long by eight feet high. The other was twenty feet long by eight high. These containers were also wide enough to either fit on the back of a railroad flatcar or on a regular freight truck.

The shipping companies then designed large cargo ships that could hold these containers. These ships looked more like oil tankers than the old-style, three-island steamers. The bridge was moved aft to open up more forward cargo room. The cargo holds were fitted with frameworks that held both types of container. When they were finished, the ship designers had a freighter

The container ship can be loaded and unloaded quickly. Some of these ships allow trucks to drive the cargo on and off the ship, eliminating the need to use cranes for loading and unloading.

that could be unloaded, reloaded, and sent back to sea within a few days. This ship, called a container ship, rapidly became the modern world's standard cargo ship. Most of the world's cargo is sent across the seas using these ships.

Another development in container shipping has also become popular. Some ships are equipped with ramps leading from one side of the ship onto the loading dock. Trucks drive the cargo directly into the ship's cargo hold. There, the cargo containers are detached and lashed down for the voy-age. At the end of the trip, the containers do not need to be unloaded by cranes. They simply are driven out of the ship to their final destination. This method is called roll-on/roll-off shipping, or ro-ro for short.

Traveling in Style

As changes in cargo ship design made shipping more dependable and affordable, passenger travel went through similar changes. The great transatlantic

Shipbuilders developed standardized containers (left) for more efficient cargo loading. The container ship (right) was specially designed to carry these containers.

passenger liners carried travelers and immigrants across the Atlantic for nearly sixty years. The speed with which these ships made the crossing and the luxury they offered passengers created an aura of glamour that fascinated the public. Many liners were built and operated by companies in the United States, Great Britain, France, Germany, and other nations. But the history of the passenger liner can be traced through the history of three memorable ships—the *Great Eastern, Mauretania,* and *Normandie.*

The first of these ships, the *Great Eastern,* was constructed in the middle of the nineteenth century.

Before the development of the steamship passenger lines, people had to travel by freight ships and were treated like second-class cargo. The sailing packets, with their regular departures, were slightly better. Still, their accommodations were crude. There were few comforts available for the passengers. And despite the packet's reputed speed, bad weather sometimes meant

the voyage took more than two months.

One main advantage of the early passenger steamships, like Isambard Brunel's *Great Western* of 1838, was their ability to arrive in port on a definite day. Steamship owners also invested in making steamship travel comfortable. They hired crews who were intelligent, courteous, and knowledgeable. Captains, too, were chosen both for their skill and their willingness to treat their passengers well.

Naturally, the atmosphere on board the steamships was more pleasant. Even so, steamships were simply holding their own against the packets until Brunel built his *Great Britain* in 1843. The fame of the iron-hulled passenger ship spurred the development of more passenger steamers. It also spurred competition among shipping lines.

Brunel was still not satisfied. He wanted to build a passenger liner that could voyage nonstop from England to Australia. Aside from the United States, the most popular destination for Europeans was Australia. That island conti-

Passenger steamships offered comfortable accommodations as well as reliable arrival times.

The passenger ship Great Eastern *was designed to be a grand seagoing hotel. Although its size was impressive, the ship was difficult to maneuver and the existing ports could barely accommodate its huge proportions.*

nent was going through a gold mining boom similar to the one in California. Thousands of immigrants each year were booking passage on the freighters and other ships that sailed from England in search of Australian gold. Brunel's fame with his prior two ships convinced the Eastern Steam Navigation Company to allow him to begin work on the gigantic steamship *Great Eastern* in 1854.

Great Eastern was Brunel's masterpiece. At almost seven hundred feet long, it was six times as large as any other ship in the world. To move the massive ship, Brunel equipped it with two side paddle wheels *and* a pair of screw propellers. This arrangement gave the ship a top speed of 14.5 knots, a little more than 16.5 miles per hour.

Obstacles to Overcome

Building the ship almost proved to be too difficult. Because of its size, the hull would not fit in a conventional dry dock. It had to be built on an island in the middle of the Thames River near London. It took three months to move the ship the few yards that separated it from the river. During that time, two men were killed. Thousands of dollars' worth of heavy moving machinery was destroyed. By the time *Great Eastern* reached the Thames, the Eastern Steam Navigation Company was bankrupt.

Great Eastern had a double-layered iron hull, which once kept the ship afloat when its outer layer was punctured. It had a flat bottom for stability. And it had a series of walls stretching from one side of the hull to another. These walls, called bulkheads, were designed to keep the ship afloat if both layers of the hull were punctured. Water would only flood one section of the ship because the bulkheads would keep the other sections dry and airtight. Doors equipped with tight rubber gaskets let sailors and passengers walk from one section to another.

Inside, the ship was an artistic triumph. *Great Eastern* pioneered the idea of a liner as a seagoing grand hotel. Its grand saloon alone contained tapestries, gold-paneled walls, and skillfully crafted furniture made of the finest wood available. The cabins, while small by today's standards, were the largest available on any ship afloat. The luxury of the ship deeply impressed its visitors, including Queen Victoria and her husband, Prince Albert.

Problems Plague *Great Eastern*

Great Eastern had its problems, however. First, the ship was simply too big for its time. Maneuvering the seagoing giant proved to be too stressful for its captains, who were used to ships a fraction of its size. They rarely commanded the ship for more than one voyage before quitting. The seaports of the world as well were nearly overwhelmed by the ship. They had to push their facilities to the limit to handle it.

Brunel died the day before the ship's maiden voyage. Some people said the stroke that killed him came from the stress of building the ship. The ship's new owners, the Great Ship Company, decided to capitalize on the public's initial excitement over the craft. Instead of offering nonstop cruises to Australia, they introduced the ship as a transatlantic liner. This was a catastrophic mistake. Smaller steamships and the few remaining sailing packets could do the same job far better than *Great Eastern*. Certainly, they were able to charge their passengers less than the gigantic ship had to.

Public interest in *Great Eastern* soon faded. No one wanted to pay premium prices for a trip they could take on a smaller, less expensive ship. In the 1860s, *Great Eastern* passed into the hands of a third company. Its interior finery was ripped out, and the ship was put to work laying underwater telegraph cables. Aside from a brief at-

The luxurious interior of the Great Eastern *impressed Queen Victoria, who toured the ship before its maiden voyage.*

tempt to restore it as a passenger liner, *Great Eastern* remained a cable-laying ship for the rest of its active life.

By 1900, smaller liners had taken up the passenger trade initiated by the *Great Eastern*. Their goal also was to provide fast, luxurious travel to transatlantic travelers. By now, compound engines with their more powerful multiple pistons were available for use at sea. All ships used the more efficient screw propeller. Together, these improvements drove the liners across the Atlantic at speeds of more than twenty knots, about twenty-three miles per hour. Such an emphasis was placed on speedy travel that the Atlantic liners began competing with each other for the fastest time. The victorious ships were awarded a trophy called the Blue Ribbon.

The Blue Ribbon was to passenger

THE TURBINE ENGINE

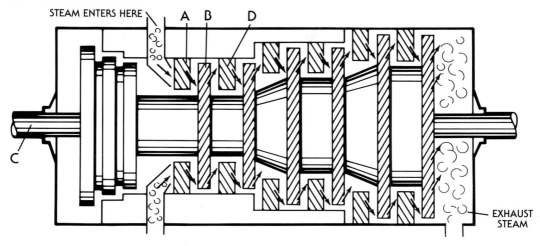

STEAM ENTERS HERE

A B D

C

EXHAUST STEAM

When the steam enters a turbine engine, it strikes a set of fixed blades (A). The blades vent the steam at an angle toward a set of rotating blades (B). As the steam strikes the rotating blades, they turn, powering the shaft (C). The rotating blades, in turn, deflect the steam at an angle toward another set of fixed blades (D). The process is repeated several times as the steam weaves its way through the engine to the exhaust.

As the steam moves through the engine, it loses pressure. Since large blades can be turned more easily than small ones, the size of the blades increases as the pressure of the steam decreases.

The turbine engine is very efficient. It uses the power of the steam to turn many sets of blades before the steam condenses. Since the turbine constantly turns in one direction, it can build up a great deal of momentum, making it even easier to turn. Once in motion, the turbine requires little energy to keep moving.

liners what the America's Cup is to modern yacht racers. The Blue Ribbon became as much of a goal to the liner's captains and owners as the comfort of the passengers. Liners were built so they could compete for this prize.

Liners were extremely narrow at the waterline in order to push aside as little water as possible. They widened at the top to accommodate passenger cabins and the bridge structure. Their hulls swept back from almost razor-sharp bows that cut apart the waves. Stream-

lining—designing the ship so air and water flowed by smoothly—became the operating principle. To heighten the sense of the liners' speed, advertising posters exaggerated their narrow head-on profiles and high hulls. People began seeing liners not as machines but as ocean greyhounds racing across the plains of the sea.

This image was strengthened when the steam turbine engines were introduced around 1900. Suddenly, ships were built that could sail as fast as twenty-five knots (roughly twenty-nine miles per hour) or more. Though slow compared with trains or automobiles, the speed was very fast for a ship. That a huge vessel full of passengers could travel so fast astounded people living at the turn of the century.

As astounding was the fact that a person could cross the Atlantic, a trip that used to take months, in less than a week. Transatlantic telephone service was still in its infancy at this time, and radio was a primitive technology. Liners brought about a revolution in communication. Through travel, people were exposed to countries and cultures that they could have only read about in the past. News, fashions, and technical advances crossed the ocean with blinding speed.

Mauretania: Romance of the Ocean Greyhounds

The most beloved of the great ocean liners was the *Mauretania*. Built in 1907 for Cunard Lines, a British company, it used the power of four turbines to turn two screw propellers. *Mauretania* and its sister ship, *Lusitania*, had been designed to dominate transatlantic voyages. From 1907 to 1939, traveling by liner was considered one of the great status symbols of the world. Liners offered the image of catering to the overseas adventurer as well as to the sightseeing tourist.

Shortly after it began service, *Mauretania* won the prized Blue Ribbon. It sailed from one side of the Atlantic to the other in only four days, ten hours, and fifty-one minutes. The ship could boast an average speed of twenty-six knots (thirty miles per hour). It was destined to hold onto the trophy for the next twenty-one years before technology allowed faster ships to be built.

But its speed was only one of the factors that won the hearts of the passengers. Travelers loved the richly decorated cabins and common areas and appreciated the competent and attentive crew. One passenger, Franklin Delano Roosevelt, summed up their feelings

The ocean liner Mauretania *was prized for its speed as well as its service and luxurious interior.*

The Normandie *'s narrow bow allowed for less water resistance and faster sailing.*

best: "Every ship has a soul. But the *Mauretania* has one you could talk to."

The soul of the *Mauretania* carried the ship through both world wars and into the early 1960s. By then, however, the "grand old lady of the Atlantic" was more than forty years old. It could no longer successfully compete with newer ships. Finally, in the late 1960s, it was sold and dismantled for scrap.

Normandie: France's Seagoing Jewel

In 1929, a French steamship line decided to build a liner larger and more luxurious than any liner before it. This company, known in the United States as the French Line, was determined to win the Blue Ribbon for France. Though the ship would weigh more than eighty thousand tons, it would be powered by a turboelectric engine. This powerful, fast, and reliable engine system had been in use on a number of American liners. The American ships, however, were never as popular as the European ships. But the owners of the French Line saw that the engine would win them the prize they sought.

Called the *Normandie*, the ship was designed by a Russian named Vladimir Yourkevitch. Yourkevitch knew that to win the Blue Ribbon, the ship would have to present a minimum amount of surface area to the surrounding sea. A decrease in surface area causes a decrease in the resistance from the water, which causes an increase in speed. Yourkevitch exaggerated the streamlined bow of the traditional liner and flared the top of the hull. Although *Normandie* was the largest passenger ship afloat and seemed as tall as a mountain, it looked as narrow and sharp as the blade of a sword when seen from the front.

Normandie was innovative on the inside as well. Specially commissioned statues, murals, and other works of art filled the ship. A full hospital with at

Although the Normandie *was the pride of France, it never had the commercial success its builders expected. Its rival, the* Queen Mary *(left), had more success attracting transatlantic passengers.*

least two doctors was also provided. Other miscellaneous comforts included an indoor swimming pool, a theater, children's playrooms, and a fifty-foot-long chapel. There was even space near the ship's bottom to carry passengers' cars or small airplanes.

With its first voyage in 1935, *Normandie* broke all records for the transatlantic run. It set an average speed of 30 knots, or 34.5 miles per hour. The ship was thought to be the first entry in a new era of magnificent liners. Transcon-tinental air travel was possible by this time. But the propeller-driven airplanes were too slow and uncomfortable for all but the hardiest travelers. Nothing could match the comfort that ships like *Normandie* offered.

The French Line never got the business it hoped for, however. In 1936, *Normandie* carried only 27,300 people across the ocean. A rival ship, the Cunard liner *Queen Mary*, carried 42,000 passengers that year. To make up for losses on the Atlantic run, *Normandie*

Today, commercial airlines have nearly replaced passenger ships as a means of transportation. The liners now accommodate those who wish to vacation aboard a luxurious, floating resort.

began off-season cruises to Brazil. Rather than ushering in a new era of liner travel, *Normandie* served as one of the last examples of glamorous sea travel. The ship itself was destroyed by fire during World War II, when it was being converted into an Allied troop ship.

The Development of the Cruise Ship

The role of passenger ships after World War II was far different than it had been before the war. No longer were ships the only way to get from one continent to another. Wartime advances in airplane engineering and design were soon incorporated into commercial airplanes. After 1945, planes could fly transcontinental routes almost without risk. By 1950, ship travel had assumed a secondary position. Only couples on their honeymoon or families on vacation wanted to spend days at sea traveling. Most people preferred the speed of the new airplanes. An air voyage across the Atlantic was measured in hours, not days. For people on a limited schedule, air travel gave them more time to spend at their destination.

It became pointless to keep build-ing ships that could trim minutes off a voyage. No ship would ever be able to beat an airplane. Instead, passenger lines began to concentrate on those people who went to sea merely to relax. These people either remembered or had read about the romance of sea travel. That was what they wanted to ex-perience on board ship.

Starting in the mid-1950s, ships were designed as floating resorts. The focus shifted toward entertaining the passengers rather than merely letting them pass the time until the voyage was over. The ship was the destination rather than the means of reaching it. In fact, no destination was necessary. The ship could merely cruise around for a week or two before returning to its home port.

Today, cruise ships have truly be-come floating hotels. Some ships offer such diversions as indoor malls with central courts more than five stories tall. Others offer conveniences like fit-ness centers with jogging tracks. The main difference between these ships and the old liners is speed. The "ocean greyhounds" of the 1930s could reach speeds above thirty knots. Today, "full speed ahead" on many cruise ships means going no faster than twenty knots.

Warships' Powerful Presence

The impact of ships on warfare has been as big, if not bigger, than their impact on trade. Until the mid-fifteenth century, for example, ships were used solely to send soldiers and supplies to foreign battlefields. At most, ships from opposing sides were used as seagoing platforms on which armies fought hand to hand. But then ships like the galleons, which were built specifically to carry large numbers of cannons, soon turned the seas themselves into battlefields.

Ships of the Line

Warships developed after the fifteenth century were based on the galleon. For a while, the galleon *was* the world's main warship. War galleons were equipped with slightly better weapons than cargo galleons and carried no treasure. It soon became clear, though, that the navies of the world needed ships designed solely as fighters.

Builders took the basic galleon design and made it bigger, adding more gun decks and making the hulls thicker to withstand enemy cannon shots. The biggest sailing warships, those with sixty or more cannons, were called ships of the line. They were called this because they could fire cannons effectively only from their sides, and so the general battle strategy was to sail one's warships in a single line toward the enemy's ships, which were also lined up. Each fleet

then fired intense volleys at the other. Ships of the line could mount a few cannons facing to the front or the rear, but these were not very accurate.

Some of the best fighting ships were those used by the Royal Navy of Great Britain. British warships both defended the nation from attack and imposed British control over the seas for nearly two hundred years. Much of Britain's colonial empire from North America to Hong Kong was kept in check through Britain's control over major shipping lanes.

One of the best-known of Britain's sail-powered warships was HMS *Victory.* The largest ship of the line ever built, *Victory* served as the flagship of Admiral Lord Horatio Nelson during the historic Battle of Trafalgar in 1805. During this battle, fought off Spain's Cape

Britain's HMS Victory *was a sail-powered warship that triumphed in the Battle of Trafalgar.*

Admiral Lord Horatio Nelson, commander of Victory, *defeated French and Spanish ships during the Battle of Trafalgar.*

Trafalgar near the Strait of Gibraltar, Nelson faced a fleet of French and Spanish ships. Nelson's strategy was revolutionary. He divided his fleet into two squadrons and sent them into the side of the enemy's line. This tactic took the French and Spanish ships by surprise, and their fleet became disorganized in trying to fight Nelson's two squadrons. By itself, *Victory* crippled the French admiral's flagship by firing more than fifty shots through the French ship's stern. This concentration of cannon fire ripped through the French ship, killing half of its crew and disabling twenty cannons. Though Nelson was killed

later in the battle, his fleet's victory assured his name as Britain's greatest admiral.

Dawn of the Ironclads

The Battle of Trafalgar was virtually the last of the great battles between wooden warships. The Royal Navy and other navies soon began developing shells that could pierce even the thickest wooden hull. To counter these weapons, navies added iron plates to their ships' hulls. At the same time, navies began experimenting with steam power, which was needed to move the heavier ships.

The development of these ironclad ships led to the quick demise of the wooden warship. The first battle of ironclad ships took place during the American Civil War. The ships USS *Monitor* and CSS *Virginia* (formerly the USS *Merrimack*) were two of the strangest-looking ships ever built.

The *Virginia* was a Confederate ship. It was built on the nearly burned-out hull of a captured steam-powered Union warship. The Confederate navy used this prize to build a nearly indestructible ironclad. A long tent-shaped iron cover was built onto the wooden hull. A single line of guns poked out of ports along both sides and the front of the ship, which was the traditional setup of a wooden warship.

Monitor, a Union ship, looked even stranger than *Virginia,* but it was a technological masterpiece. Its designer was John Ericsson, a Swedish engineer who immigrated to the United States before the war began. One sailor described the ship Ericsson built as a "floating water tank." It had a flat, oval-shaped iron hull that rose only a few inches above the waterline. In the center of the ship was a short, covered metal cylinder that could turn in a full circle. Inside, it housed two short, powerful guns. The structure was called a gun turret. At a time when ships fought by firing volleys from all the guns poking through one side of the ship, this turret was a marvel. It allowed a ship to fire its guns in any direction, rather than forcing it to line up with an enemy target. Later, turrets were to become standard on warships around the world. At the time *Monitor* was built, however, many people were skeptical about its ability to perform during battle.

Actually, both vessels had their drawbacks. Their engines burned too much fuel to make long solo journeys practical. Often, *Virginia* had to be towed to its battle sites. They were also slow, with a maximum speed of six or seven knots. The first battle between the ironclads took place on March 9,

1862, while the *Virginia* was attacking Union ships just off the Virginia shore, near the town of Hampton.

Strangely enough, neither ship won the fight. *Virginia*'s shots mostly passed over the flat hull of the Union ship. The shots that did hit the hull bounced off, causing little or no damage. The same thing happened when *Monitor* tried to attack *Virginia*. *Virginia*'s armor was too thick for the light, slow-moving cannon fire. The battle ended when both ships withdrew and steamed in opposite directions.

Though neither ship won the fight, *Monitor* did win the design war. *Virginia*'s fixed guns had proved useless in the face of *Monitor*'s turret guns, which could fire at its Confederate rival from any direction. *Virginia*, on the other hand, could fire only when its target was directly in front of its guns.

Neither ship would fight again. In May, *Virginia*'s crew sank the ship as it was about to be recaptured by Union

The American Civil War featured the first battle between ironclad ships. Here, the Confederate's CSS Virginia *battles the Union's USS* Monitor.

After the Monitor *sank, the United States built other ships called monitors. The* Onondaga *(left) was a monitor that implemented the gun turret.*

forces. *Monitor* was sunk during a hurricane in December. After the *Monitor* sank, the United States ordered more of the tank-shaped ships, which were called monitors.

Ironclads and Battleships

After the Battle of Hampton Roads, the age of wooden warships was over. Ironclads would have no trouble demolishing even the strongest wooden battleship.

But warship development between 1865 and the 1890s was a slow, experimental process. Though navies soon realized that an all-iron or all-steel ship would be faster and more sturdy than ironclad wood, builders clung to many of the design features of sailing ships, which made the ironclads less effective. They were unsure of the best way to build the new ships. Even though they were steam-powered, ironclads built after the Civil War still carried sails. Masts and rigging cluttered a ship's upper deck. They made the task of handling the ship in combat difficult. The ironclads also used paddle wheels. Mounted on the outside of the ship's hull, paddle wheels were vulnerable to enemy guns.

The ironclads of the late nineteenth century were less efficient than they could have been because shipbuilders still built them like sailing ships.

Battleships were built with thick iron or steel armor for protection during war.

No one could or would pass up such an easy target. One or two good hits could leave an ironclad dead in the water.

Finally, most navies were reluctant to abandon the familiar broadside gun pattern. They tried to mount their turrets so that all guns could fire from one side of the ship or the other. One spectacularly unsuccessful design had two turrets mounted in an open hold just above the ship's waterline, allowing for traditional combat. The ship sank when heavy seas washed into the vessel through open or faulty hatches in the gun deck.

These problems were solved in the 1870s, a decade that marked the con-struction of truly modern warships. One of the first of these vessels was the British warship HMS *Devastation*, launched in 1873. The design of the ship was a bold step for the Royal Navy. *Devastation* had no sails to supplement or take over for the steam engine. It discarded the paddle wheel for a screw propeller. And it had four guns mounted in two turrets fore and aft of the bridge structure. After more than three hundred years, the traditional broadside design was gone.

Devastation was the world's first modern battleship. It and other early battleships were protected with ten or more inches of iron or steel armor. The extra weight meant the battleships could not go much faster than twenty knots. But the extra protection made the ship almost impossible to destroy—except by another battleship.

The Cruiser

Soon after the first battleships were built, a second type of warship appeared. This ship was called the cruiser. It was designed as an independent patrol ship that could "cruise" the seas. Its

The cruiser was originally built to protect merchant ships and scout war fleets. Later, navies built armored cruisers such as this one as battleships.

original duties were to protect merchant ships and to act as a scout for war fleets. At first, the cruiser was armed with only a few powerful guns. Though it was metal-hulled, it did not carry any armor. Instead, it relied on speed for defense. Its designers planned for it to be too fast to hit.

As time went on, the world's major navies began building larger cruisers. The idea was to use cruisers as fast battleships, again substituting speed for armor. These cruisers had guns that could fire shells as thick as ten inches or more. Eventually, some of the cruisers were built with a few inches of armor. These were called protected or armored cruisers. The very largest were called battle cruisers.

Mahan and the Great Fleets

By the 1900s, many of the world's major powers were still deciding how many of each type of ship they needed. In the United States, in particular, politicians and naval officers argued over whether to build a large battleship navy or a smaller force featuring cruisers. Then in 1890, a book called *The Influence of Seapower on History* was published. It gave support to the large-ship navy. The book's author, Rear Admiral Alfred Thayer Mahan, said that large, modern navies were essential for nations that wanted to be world powers. He pointed to battles like the one near Cape Trafalgar as examples of how strong navies maintain a nation's international power.

Mahan's book spurred the development of big battleships in navies around the world. The most notable of these new fleets was the Great White Fleet of

Rear Admiral Alfred Thayer Mahan adhered to the theory that a large, strong navy is necessary to maintain political power.

the United States. This fleet—twenty-six battleships and smaller craft painted white as a sign of peace—sailed around the world from 1907 to 1909. The voyage had been ordered by President Theodore Roosevelt as a display of U.S. military and political might.

HMS *Dreadnought*

The most notable example of shipbuilding influenced by Mahan's book was HMS *Dreadnought*, built in 1906. *Dreadnought* was the world's most heavily armed warship. It carried ten guns with barrels measuring twelve inches in diameter. These guns were mounted in five turrets around the ship, in a pattern allowing the ship to fire six or eight guns at a time in any direction. In contrast, earlier battleships mixed twelve-inch guns with smaller weapons, yielding far less firepower than what *Dreadnought*'s guns offered.

In addition to its big guns, *Dreadnought* was armed with smaller guns and torpedo tubes. Its 561-foot-long hull was lined with eleven-inch-thick armor. And it had steam turbine engines, the first ever used in a battleship, that propelled it at twenty-one knots, or twenty-four miles per hour, faster than any other battleship afloat. *Dreadnought* was so impressive that Britain and other nations soon built more like it. These ships became known as dreadnoughts in honor of the revolutionary ship that inspired them. They carried even heavier weaponry than the original, with fifteen-inch guns common by 1915.

Warships of World War I

The sea battles of World War I featured early versions of all the warships that make up most of the world's navies today. Battleships and cruisers were the main ships used by Great Britain, Germany, and the United States. But only the battleship proved to be an effective warship. Cruisers, especially the battle cruisers, were too lightly armed and armored to be of much use as fighters. The idea that cruisers would be fast enough to outrun enemy ships and gunfire proved false. Most of the ships that were lost in combat during World War I were cruisers.

Battleships and cruisers were not the only ships in use at the time, however. The Royal Navy had developed two smaller vessels that were to play larger roles during and after World War II. The first was the destroyer, a fast ship designed to fend off attack from torpedo boats. Torpedo boats were long, fast boats or small ships armed with self-propelled torpedoes. (The original "torpedo" was an explosive charge at the end of a long pole mounted on the front of a boat.) Traveling at nineteen knots or more, the torpedo boats attacked ships sailing in line or resting at anchor. The British destroyers were fast enough to block and attack torpedo boats before the boats could reach the larger ships. Destroyers were also armed with torpedoes and could attack larger enemy ships if necessary.

The destroyer made early torpedo boats obsolete. (In World War II, however, the United States built faster, more agile torpedo boats that were very effective in sinking Japanese freighters and warships.) In their place, submarines were developed. The German U-boat, especially, was a terrifying foe to surface ships. The submarines could remain submerged and unseen while they waited for their targets to line up with their torpedoes. The first clue a ship's crew often had that a submarine was

The German U-boat could remain submerged and unseen as it scouted out the enemy with a periscope that peered out above the water.

During World War I, planes were used to seek out enemy fleets. The planes, however, were slow and often far from the battle site. These limitations led to the invention of aircraft carriers which could carry and launch airplanes from sea.

tracking it was when the first torpedo blew up under the hull.

British and, later, American destroyers were soon adapted for antisubmarine combat. Destroyers were able to exploit the disadvantages of U-boats. U-boats needed time to get into position to fire their torpedoes, and the only way to aim the torpedoes was for an officer to look through a periscope that poked above the waves. Sharp-eyed surface seamen were constantly on the lookout for this telltale sign that a submarine was nearby. Once the submarine was spotted, the destroyer would attack it with torpedoes or depth charges. A depth charge is an antisubmarine bomb dropped off the side or stern of a ship. It is set to explode when it reaches the target submarine's depth.

The other vessel developed by Britain was a forerunner of the modern aircraft carrier. Airplanes long had held the interest of both the U.S. Navy and the Royal Navy as a means of seeking out enemy ships in wartime. (Ship-detection devices like radar and sonar would not be perfected until World War II.) During World War I, the only way to find enemy fleets was to send out a fast ship to look for them. An airplane, however, could spot the enemy without risking ships. But the planes of the time were slow and had a very short flying range. The British came up with the idea of transporting planes out to sea via ship.

Great Britain built one of the earliest aircraft carriers, H.M.S. *Ark Royal*, in 1914. *Ark Royal* was a small ship with a platform covering part of its hull. This platform was used to launch and re-

The German navy relied upon the U-boat to destroy U.S. and British warships during World War II. Here, a German U-boat undergoes attack from enemy forces.

cover small scouting biplanes. The two or three small aircraft carriers used during World War I were support ships for battleship fleets. But they were successful enough at detecting enemy ships for Great Britain and the United States to build larger carriers after the war.

Warships of World War II

The ships in the world's navies in World War II were drastically different from those of World War I. A 1922 arms restriction treaty signed in Washington, D.C., had limited the number of battleships and battle cruisers each of the five major powers of the time could have. The United States, Great Britain, Japan, France, and Italy agreed to abide by the conditions of the treaty, called the Treaty for the Limitation of Armaments. The treaty was in effect for only ten years. Even so, it began the shift in emphasis from heavily gunned warships to aircraft carriers, destroyers, and submarines.

The destroyer and the aircraft carrier became the important surface warships of World War II. In the Atlantic Ocean, Germany again relied on the deadly U-boats to disrupt commercial shipping and to destroy U.S. and British warships. Battleships were effectively useless against these hidden "wolves of the sea." Destroyers once more protected shipping in the Atlantic Ocean.

U.S. Fleets Change After Pearl Harbor

The Japanese attack on the military base in Pearl Harbor, Hawaii, in 1941 changed U.S. battle strategy. Because Japan had destroyed or disabled most

American battleships burn after the Japanese attack at Pearl Harbor, Hawaii. Because many U.S. battleships were destroyed in the attack, the navy had to depend heavily on aircraft carriers to launch warplanes to destroy enemy ships.

The Battle of Midway was largely fought by Japanese and American warplanes. The USS Enterprise *(below) during the Battle of Midway.*

of the American battleships in the Pacific, the navy switched to relying on its aircraft carriers, which had not been in port when the attack took place. The United States began attacking warships with airplanes, rather than engaging in ship-to-ship combat. By this time, wood-and-fabric biplanes had given way to metal single-winged airplanes. Many of these planes carried bombs or torpedoes for destroying ships. Others were armed strictly as fighters. These fighter planes acted as escorts for the bombing or torpedo planes and protected their fleets of warships from airplane attack. The importance of naval air power was shown during two sea battles in 1942.

The Coral Sea is an area of the South Pacific Ocean between New Guinea and the Solomon Islands. Japan had planned to invade New Guinea in May 1942 as part of its invasion of the Pacific. Fortunately, the United States found out about the planned invasion. It sent a fleet of aircraft carriers, cruisers, and other ships to intercept the Japanese warships. On May 7 and 8, the two fleets battled in the Coral Sea. But this battle was unlike any other fight at sea. For the first time in history, the battling fleets did not come in sight of each other. The actual fighting was done by the airplanes associated with each fleet.

The Battle of the Coral Sea halted Japan's advance through the Pacific. The Battle of Midway, another airplane battle, crippled the Japanese navy. Midway is an island more or less halfway between North America and Asia. Japan had planned to invade that island and lure the U.S. Navy's Pacific Fleet to its destruction. Once again, the United States found out about the plan and was able to counter Japan's move. Airplanes sank four Japanese aircraft carriers and one heavy cruiser. They also severely

A World War II U.S. torpedo bomber lands on an aircraft carrier after a strike against enemy forces.

The Modern War Fleet

The pattern established in the Pacific Ocean during World War II has held up to today. The navies of the United States, the Commonwealth of Independent States (the former Soviet Union), and other major powers base their fleets around one or two aircraft carriers. These carriers are far larger than those used in the 1940s. They have larger, angled flight decks that allow planes to take off and land at the same time. Modern carriers also use powerful steam catapults to propel their planes into the air. Carriers maintain helicopters to rescue pilots who have to eject from their planes and to detect and destroy enemy submarines. Carriers even have propeller-driven radar surveillance craft, such as the E-2 Hawkeye, to help coordinate naval air strikes.

damaged a Japanese battleship and three destroyers. This stunning victory proved that battleships no longer would be the world's main warship. Air power provided by aircraft carriers would form the core of the modern surface navy.

Because of the effectiveness of aircraft carriers, most people thought that

The aircraft carriers of today are much larger than those built during World War II. They carry several types of planes and helicopters which can take off from and land on different runways simultaneously.

The U.S. military used modernized World War II battleships during the Persian Gulf War. Here, the USS Wisconsin *fires a cruise missile at the onset of Operation Desert Storm.*

battleships had outlived their usefulness. Because battleships need to get within twenty miles of a target for their guns to be effective, they are vulnerable to attack by any carrier aircraft. For more than twenty-five years, the remaining battleships of the world sat in storage yards. But in the late 1970s, the U.S. Navy decided that battleships deserved a second look. Their big guns would be very effective in supporting troop landings on hostile beaches. And their thick armor made them virtually invulnerable to any modern bombs or missiles. The only thing that could destroy them, in fact, were torpedoes or nuclear warheads.

In 1983, the navy pulled the USS *New Jersey* out of storage. This battleship had been built in 1943. It had nine guns that could fire sixteen-inch shells more than twenty miles. But it needed some work before it could be sent back into service. Its equipment was updated with computers, satellite navigation systems, and other devices. Its big guns were supplemented with cruise missiles

that could travel far beyond the reach of the ship's shells.

The first use of this "new" battleship came during 1983 and 1984 off the coast of Lebanon. Its guns provided artillery support for a group of U.S. Marines sent as a peacekeeping force to Lebanon's capital city, Beirut. The success of the mission encouraged the modernization of three other World War II battleships: *Iowa, Missouri,* and *Wisconsin.* However, these four battleships have proven to be very expensive to operate. The battleship U.S.S. *Missouri,* which fired on targets in Iraq during the Persian Gulf War, was scheduled to go back into storage in the spring of 1992.

Though battle cruisers proved ineffective in both world wars, smaller and faster cruisers are being used for fleet surface and air defense. Modern cruisers carry surface-to-air, surface-to-surface, and cruise missiles. They also have one or two small, five-inch guns for close combat or shore bombardments.

Destroyers are used mainly for fleet defense and independent antisubmarine warfare. Modern attack and missile submarines can stay submerged for months at a time. Both types are far faster and quieter than submarines before the 1950s. They are harder for destroyers to find. Much of a destroyer's equipment includes sensitive listening devices that use computers to analyze underwater sounds. Destroyers also carry more powerful sonar detectors that can lock onto a target submarine.

Aside from hunting for submarines, destroyers can attack surface ships with torpedoes, missiles, and guns. One particularly small, fast type of destroyer is called the frigate. These ships are somewhat less expensive than full-size destroyers. Even so, they carry a formidable assortment of missiles and guns. Many smaller countries use frigates as their main, or only, warships.

Of course, there are other types of warships besides carriers, battleships, cruisers, and destroyers. The world's navies also include fast missile-carrying patrol boats, troop-carrying landing craft, and even supply ships.

Nuclear power has had limited suc-cess as a means for powering warships. Nuclear power allows ships to sail for years before they have to be refueled. Nuclear engines have two big disadvantages, however. They are far more expensive than steam, diesel, or other types of engines. They also require a great deal of heavy shielding to protect the crew from hazardous nuclear radiation. This shielding makes it far heavier than other types of engines.

These problems have forced the world's navies to limit their use of nuclear power. Only important or vital surface ships—such as aircraft carriers—have been equipped with nuclear power plants. In the U.S. Navy, only seven aircraft carriers, nine cruisers, and one destroyer are nuclear-powered. In contrast, nuclear plants have proved to be excellent power sources for submarines. They are far quieter than other engines. This is important because silence has always been the submarine's main defense. Even better, nuclear plants are self-contained. Nuclear-powered submarines do not need to surface or risk raising air tubes to get oxygen for their engines.

The Future of Ships

Ship designs are still evolving to meet the needs of shipping line owners. Most of the innovations in ship design have affected cargo ships and cruise ships. Structurally, warships have not changed a great deal since the 1960s, although there have been advances in naval weapons systems, engine design, and high-technology information processing. The shape of a warship's bridge may change, but its hull has essentially stayed the same.

Cargo Ships: Forward into the Past

International trade will always be the domain of the world's shipping industry. Some air carriers specialize in freight delivery, and many companies even concentrate on providing rapid overnight or next-day deliveries. The type and amount of cargo they can deliver, however, is limited. Airplanes are not able to transport all the world's necessities. Cargo ships can and always will be able to carry more goods for a lower price than airplanes can.

The problem the world's cargo ships are facing right now is how to make their business more economical. Fuel prices are far higher than they were when the container ship first appeared on the high seas. Aside from maintenance, fuel is one of the highest costs a shipping company has to pay. The past decade has seen a rise in a new form of ship construction that may help reduce this cost. Interestingly, this

The high cost of fuel makes cargo ships like this one expensive to operate. Consequently, new ships are being designed to make cargo shipping more economical.

new technology took its cue from the early days of steam shipping.

Cargo steamships in the late 1800s combined mechanical power with sails. On some ships, these sails were kept for emergencies only. Occasionally, they would be used to conserve a ship's fuel supply. In the 1900s, cheaper fuel and more efficient engines eliminated the need for backup sails. In the 1970s, however, rising fuel prices made shipping companies take a new look at sail power. Sails could never replace mechanical power, of course. But sails could take some of the burden off a ship's engines.

One of the leaders in the development of this new sail technology was the Japan Machinery Development Association (JAMDA). JAMDA, a commercial industry support group, encouraged shipping companies to develop new types of sails. Western nations like the United States and Germany had already experimented with rigging sails on seagoing ships. Their work had yielded mixed results—the sails saved fuel, but the cost to install them was as high as the cost of the fuel they saved. Eventually, these experiments were dropped.

JAMDA officials advocated taking a different approach. Sails may not be practical on large ships, but how about on coastal traders? A conglomerate of heavy-industry companies called Nippon Kokan Corporation (NKK) conducted tests on sail power. NKK ran computer simulations and wind-tunnel tests on different sail shapes. It also built a small oil tanker to test the best sail designs.

The results were highly unusual. The best sail for the job was not a carrack-style square sail. It was not a triangular lateen. Instead, the sail the tests showed worked best looked like a rectangular airplane wing. It was made of canvas stretched over a sturdy metal frame. The sail was curved slightly to make a wing shape. It was attached to a mast that could pivot to find the best angle for the sail. When angled to catch the wind, the sail created the same lifting force an airplane wing generates. The only difference was that this wing helped the ship "fly" on its side.

Convincing Shipbuilders to Use the New Design

JAMDA brought the result of NKK's experiments to the attention of Japan's shipping companies. At first, the idea met with a great deal of resistance. Shipowners were worried about running with sails in the stormy seas around Japan. Typhoons were a major problem. Every year, these storms force ships to seek shelter in protected harbors. How well could a sail-bearing ship withstand one of these titanic storms?

The shipowners also wondered how well the ship would perform. Would they be able to meet their schedules, or would the sails keep breaking down? The more the sails malfunctioned, the more time the ships would spend in port. A few mishaps like that could ruin a shipping company.

In the end, a few companies decided to risk building and using sail-equipped ships. They were attracted to the idea of saving money on the fuel they had to buy. Since they based their fees on oil costs, any savings were pure profit.

The first company to run a sail-equipped coastal ship was a Tokyo firm, the Aitoku Company. The company decided to commission a small tanker with a pair of rigid, rectangular sails. The *Shin Aitoku Maru* went into service in the early 1980s. By 1986, it had proved that the shipowners had no cause for their worries.

Shin Aitoku Maru sailed through storms with winds as high as seventy-five miles an hour. It met its schedules for three years with no major breakdowns. Best of all, its fuel savings nearly paid for the cost of the sails. Using the sails less than two-thirds of the time, the ship reduced its fuel consumption by 20 percent. On a ship like *Shin Aitoku Maru*, that figure can equal half a ton of fuel a day. The final cost to the Aitoku Company was less than eighty-five hundred dollars a year. This cost was acceptable because the ship proved more reliable and required less maintenance than other ships.

A New Age of Sailing Traders?

Other companies soon began building sail-assisted ships as well. The biggest of these was a transpacific cargo carrier called the *Usuki Pioneer*. This twenty-six-thousand-ton ship was designed to carry timber products and grain from North America to Japan. Its construction was a tribute to JAMDA's power of persuasion. The association convinced a group of Japanese businesses that the ship would use half the fuel of a regular ship its size. *Usuki Pioneer* has been sailing for six years now. Although it has been successful, it remains to be seen whether it will live up to JAMDA's promise.

If *Usuki Pioneer* and other ships of its type prove to be successful, they could usher in a new age of sailing traders. By using less fuel, cargo ships would even-

tually be able to charge less for their services. With lower shipping costs, the costs of imports could fall as well.

Jacques Cousteau's Cylindrical Sail

An interesting development in sail-assisted ships came from a French scientist's interpretation of a German sail design. In 1925, German engineer Anton Flettner had an idea for a bizarre ship that looked like a small cargo carrier except for one radical difference. On the bow and stern, he built a set of fifty-five-foot-high metal tubes. These tubes were made out of a special light yet strong alloy. As remarkable as it seemed, the tubes were designed to act like sails.

The tubes were mounted on a base that let them rotate to the left or right

Marine scientist Jacques-Yves Cousteau invented an efficient sail based on Anton Flettner's 1925 cylindrical sail. Cousteau called his model the Turbosail.

as the wind blew against them. The rotation built up areas of low pressure on one side of the cylinders. In effect, the rotating cylinders duplicated the mechanics of the fore-and-aft sail. The cylinders were pulled in the direction of the low-pressure zone. They, in turn, pulled the ship along.

As with the rectangular sails of the *Shin Aitoku Maru*, Flettner's cylinders were designed as supplements to mechanical power. Unfortunately, people in the 1920s were not concerned with fuel economy. Besides, they felt sails of any type belonged either to pleasure craft or to the past. They certainly did not belong on cargo ships.

The design was rediscovered by French marine scientist and explorer Jacques-Yves Cousteau in the 1970s. He saw in Lettner's failed design an idea for a different method of sail-assisted motor sailing.

A big problem with the rotating cylinder was that it kept breaking down. Cousteau thought he saw a way to solve this problem. Instead of having the cylinder turn, he kept it fixed in one place. A pair of vents ran along the side of the cylinder from top to bottom. At

Cousteau's first Turbosail-powered ship was the Moulin a vent. *Unfortunately, a cracked cylinder cut short the* Moulin a vent*'s transatlantic exhibition.*

any time, one of the vents was covered by a metal flap that was controlled by a computer. A small fan at the top of the hollow tube sucked air in through the uncovered vent. The suction created the low pressure needed for the cylinder, which Cousteau called a Turbosail, to work.

The first Turbosail ship Cousteau built, *Moulin a vent*, was a qualified success. It left the port of Tangier in Morocco on a transatlantic trip to New York. A month into the journey, rough seas and fifty-knot winds knocked the

The Alcyone, *Cousteau's wind-powered ship without sails, cuts down on fuel costs.*

cylinder off the ship. Until then, the Turbosail had worked well. It had taken the ship up to speeds of ten knots at one time. The strain on the cylinder, however, had cracked the welds at the bottom of the cylinder. A quick repair job lasted only until the ship sailed past Bermuda.

Undaunted, Cousteau built a second Turbosail ship, *Alcyone*. It was actually a joint venture between the Cousteau Society and Pechiney, a French metal company. The experimental craft had two Turbosails instead of one. It also had a pair of diesel engines for times when there was no wind. In 1985, Cousteau sailed the ship around the world to publicize the craft.

Alcyone seems to have lived up to Cousteau's expectations. It has managed to cut its fuel use by at least 15 percent in the past six years. Right now, it is one of Cousteau's two main exploration vessels. The other ship, of course, is the world-famous *Calypso*.

Cruising to the Future

Cruise ships have long been accustomed to their role as entertainment vehicles rather than serious passenger liners. Airlines still control most international passenger travel. This situation is likely to stay the same well into the next century. But cruise lines are planning to dazzle the world with their next generation of sailing resorts. They have already pushed ahead with designs that seem to belong in space rather than on the ocean.

One revolutionary design being

Sovereign of the Seas is currently the world's largest cruise ship. This seventy-four thousand ton ship can carry up to 2,690 passengers.

considered is a fifty-six-hundred-passenger ship that has its own built-in harbor. The *Phoenix World City*, if built, would be three times larger than the current largest ship, *Sovereign of the Seas*. Its hull would be split apart at the stern. This area would form a sort of bay for four smaller ships that could carry four hundred people each. These ships would probably look like the ferries that cross the lakes and harbors of the world.

Passengers on *World City* would live in one of three eight-story hotels built on top of its hull. The comforts they would enjoy might include a lagoon with sand beaches and live palm trees. As unbelievable as this ship sounds, its construction is already underway. A group of shipbuilding companies in Germany agreed in 1988 to combine their forces and build the ship.

An even more fantastic concept being considered is the Small Waterplane Area Twin Hull (SWATH) cruise ship. SWATH's design is the creation of Wartsila Marine, a shipbuilding company in Finland. If constructed, the SWATH would look unlike any ship ever built. Instead of a conventional hull, it would have two underwater pontoons. A pontoon is a metal cylinder normally used to hold up floating bridges. The ship would rest on huge metal struts connecting it to the pontoons. Wartsila Marine thinks this arrangement would lift the platform of the ship above the waves. This way, it would be less vulnerable to surface turbulence.

The SWATH would not rest on a regular V-shaped hull. Therefore, it could be built more like a seagoing building than like a normal ship. One plan being considered has the ship measuring five hundred feet long by two hundred feet wide. Seen from above, the ship would look like an arrowhead. Inside, it could have an exposed recreation area measuring more than thirty thousand square feet.

Other cruise ship designs being considered range from glass towers mounted on triple hulls to islands complete with tennis courts, small boat docks, and an amusement park. Cruise lines hope these innovative designs will keep attracting passengers well into the next century.

Today, ships are no longer the primary means of international travel. But the growth and maintenance of trade among countries depends on having enough advanced cargo-carrying ships to haul goods. Shipbuilders constantly seek for ways ships can carry more goods while using as little fuel as possible. And, as the decades progress, the ships that were used in the past two decades will seem as old-fashioned as those used in the previous two centuries.

Glossary

■■

aft: The rear end of a ship or a boat.

age of discovery: Period between 1400 and 1600 when Western nations began seeking out trade routes to the Far East.

amidships: The middle of a ship or a boat.

batten: Strip of wood used to keep a sail flat in the wind. Battens were also used to tighten canvas hatch covers, hence the phrase "batten down the hatches."

beating: To sail against the wind.

before the wind: Sailing with the wind coming directly over the rear of one's ship.

bow: The forward end of a ship or a boat.

canoe: Narrow boat, usually with pointed ends, made of skin, bark, or hollowed-out tree trunks.

caravel: Sailing ship with a carvel-built hull, a stern-hung rudder, and two or more masts hung with lateen sails; first built in Portugal in the early fifteenth century.

carvel-built: Wooden boat or ship hull made with planks joined edge to edge.

carrack: The first ship to combine square and lateen sails, which allowed the ship to sail in virtually any weather. The ship also had a carvel-built hull, a stern hung rudder, and a forecastle and aftercastle hanging over the bow and stern; first built in the mid-fifteenth century.

clinker-built: Wooden boat or ship hull made with planks that overlap top to bottom.

clipper: Fast, narrow cargo ship designed to "clip" short the time it took to sail certain trade routes. Clippers were most easily identified by the large amounts of sail they carried in their masts.

cog: Short, round sailing ship with one square sail. The cog was the main ship used in the Middle Ages.

container ship: Twentieth-century cargo ship that transports goods inside rectangular metal boxes.

deck: Any of the horizontal platforms on a ship that form floors and ceilings; also, the space defined by two of these platforms.

diesel: Form of refined oil that can be burned and used like gasoline; also, the engine invented by Rudolf Diesel that uses this fuel.

donkey engine: Small, powerful, multi-purpose engine often used to power heavy-duty winches.

dugout: Canoe made by hollowing out a section of tree trunk.

fluyt: Dutch trading ship of the seventeenth century; also known as a flyboat.

fore: The forward end of a ship or a boat.

fore-and-aft sail: Sail that points along the line of a ship's keel, such as the lateen sail and the Chinese lugsail.

forecastle: Originally, a fighting platform attached to the bow of a ship; now, the forward part of any ship.

freeboard: The distance between the top of a ship's hull and the waterline.

galley: Long, narrow warship propelled by rows of human-powered oars. Its main weapon was a metal ram fixed to the bow of the ship. The galley was the main fighting ship of the Mediterranean Sea until the late 1500s.

galleon: Combination cargo ship and warship developed in the sixteenth century. It was first used by Spain to guard its treasure fleets in the New World.

helm: Ship's steering controls.

hull: The outer portion of the body of a ship or a boat.

Indiaman: Sailing ship designed especially for the Europe-to-India trade route. Indiamen were designed and painted to look like warships to ward off pirates and the ships of enemy countries.

ironclad: Early metal-hulled, metal-armored, steam-powered warship.

junk: Ship with lugsails that was developed in China.

keel: The central supporting member of a ship's frame. It is made of wood or metal and runs the length of the ship.

knarr: Large sailing ship used as a merchant vessel by the Vikings.

knot: Measure of a ship's speed. One knot is equal to one nautical mile per hour.

lateen sail: Sail shaped like a triangle that allows ships to sail close to the wind.

liner: Passenger ship devoted to providing travelers with luxurious passage over the ocean.

longboat: Sail- and oar-driven ship used by the Vikings during their raids on European coastal towns and seaports.

lugsail: Four-cornered, triangular-shaped sail stiffened with wooden strips. It was developed for use on Chinese junks.

mate: Officer on board a merchant ship.

mizzen: Mast on a carrack or a galleon that carried a lateen sail.

nautical mile: Distance equal to roughly 6,080 feet.

packet ship: Sailing ship of the early 1800s that carried passengers and mail across the Atlantic Ocean and made regular, scheduled departures.

paddle wheel: Large wheel made up of individual planks connected to a central axis. As the wheels dug into the water, the ship was forced forward.

port: The left side of a ship or a boat; also, a harbor or other facility for ships that are not at sea.

reaching: Sailing at a diagonal to the direction the wind is blowing.

rib: Support for a ship's hull that is attached to the ship's keel.

rudder: Flat piece of wood or metal used to steer a ship or a boat.

running: Sailing before the wind.

sail: Large, flat surface designed to use the power of the wind to move a ship or a boat. Most sails are made of canvas, nylon, or some other fabric. Recently, cargo ships have begun experimenting with sails made of metal or of canvas on metal frames.

screw propeller: Device made of metal vanes attached to a central axis. As the propeller turns, it seems to screw its way through the water.

shell-built construction: Shipbuilding method in which the hull of the ship is constructed before any ribs are installed.

skeleton-built construction: Shipbuilding method in which hull planks or plates are attached to a pre-assembled frame in the shape of a ship.

spar: Long pole used to support a sail as it hangs from a mast.

starboard: The right side of a ship.

steam engine: Engine that converts the heat and pressure of steam into mechanical work.

stem: The forward end of a ship or a boat.

stern: The rear end of a ship or a boat.

tacking: Sailing against the wind by zigzagging across it.

tiller: Long steering pole attached to the rudder of a ship or a boat.

turbine: Wheel made up of or covered with small vanes that is turned by steam pressure to produce power; also, an engine that uses turbines.

turbosail: Rotating cylinder that is designed to act like a sail made of fabric.

Viking: Any one of several groups of Scandinavian raiders and explorers who were active in the eighth, ninth, and tenth centuries.

westerlies: Zone of winds that blow constantly from west to east.

For Further Reading

William C. Heine, *Historic Ships of the World.* New York: Putnam's, 1977.

A. A. and Mary Hoehling, *The Last Voyage of the Lusitania.* New York: Henry Holt, 1956.

Barry Jacobs, "The Saga of *Great Eastern,* " *Oceans,* January/February 1980.

Allan E. Jordan, "Superships," *Popular Mechanics,* December 1988.

Douglas Lobley, *Ships Through the Ages.* London: Octopus Books, 1972.

Works Consulted

Harry Basch and Shirley Slater, "Cruising into the 1990s," *Travel-Holiday*, December 1989.

Bernard Brett, *The History of Seapower*. New York: The Military Press, 1985.

Graham Cooper, "Ships of the Future," *World Press Review*, June 1986.

Bernard Ireland, *Warships from Sail to the Nuclear Age*. London: Hamlyn, 1978.

Paul Johnstone, *The Sea-Craft of Prehistory*. Edited by Sean McGrail. Cambridge: Harvard University Press, 1980.

Edward V. Lewis, Robert O'Brien, and the editors of *Life* Magazine, *Ships*. New York: Time, Inc., 1965.

Michael W. Marshall, *Ocean Traders: From the Portuguese Discoveries to the Present Day*. New York: Facts on File, 1990.

James M. Morris, *History of the U.S. Navy*. New York: Exeter Books, 1984.

New Orleans, "Ro-Ros: The Future Rolls On for the Port of New Orleans," January 1984.

J. H. Parry, *Romance of the Sea*. Washington, DC: National Geographic Society, 1981.

Sail, "Cousteau Loses Experimental Rig in the Atlantic," February 1984.

Randy Thomas, "Freighters Under Sail," *Oceans*, May/June 1986.

Tre Tryckare, *The Lore of Ships*. New York: Holt, Rinehart & Winston, 1963.

Barbara W. Tuchman, *The First Salute*. New York: Knopf, 1988.

David Wallechinsky and Irving Wallace, *The People's Almanac*. Garden City, NY: Doubleday, 1975.

The World Atlas of Archaeology. New York: Portland House, 1985.

Yachting, "Cousteau/Pechiney Turboship," October 1985.

Index

About the Author

Free-lance writer Sean M. Grady is the youngest writer for *The Encyclopedia of Discovery and Invention.* Originally a physics major, he received a Bachelor of Arts degree in print journalism from the University of Southern California in 1988. While in college, he worked for the entertainment section of the *Los Angeles Times* as a reporting intern; for *California Magazine* as a research intern; and for the City News Service of Los Angeles, a local news wire, as a general assignment reporter. In the two years after his graduation, Mr. Grady specialized in business reporting and worked as business editor of *The Olympian,* a daily newspaper in Olympia, Washington. Mr. Grady currently lives in Sparks, Nevada.

Picture Credits

■■

Cover photo by FPG

AP/Wide World Photos, 36, 63, 76 (bottom), 77

The Bettmann Archive, 15, 22, 24 (bottom), 41, 42, 44, 47 (both), 58, 67, 69 (bottom)

Bettmann/Hulton, 66

Bob Caldwell, 21, 25, 46, 52, 54, 61

Consulate General of Japan, N.Y., 79

Library of Congress, 13 (both), 18 (both), 27 (both), 28 (both), 29 (both), 31, 32, 37 (bottom), 59, 62, 71, 72

National Archives, 40 (top), 68, 69 (top), 70 (both), 74 (both), 75 (both), 76 (top)

San Diego Maritime Museum, 43, 51, 53

Smithsonian Institution, 45, 73

Stock Montage/Historical Pictures Services, 12, 14, 19, 20, 23, 24 (top), 26, 33, 34, 35, 37 (top), 38, 39 (bottom), 40 (bottom), 48, 49, 50, 60

Tim Sunderman, 16, 17

UPI/Bettmann, 64 (bottom right), 81, 82 (both), 83

© Vision Impact Photolibrary, 55 (both), 57 (all), 64 (top, bottom left)